A FIELD OF TELEPHONES

Zach Savich

Also by Zach Savich

Poetry

Full Catastrophe Living (2009)
Annulments (2010)
The Firestorm (2011)
Century Swept Brutal (2014)
The Orchard Green and Every Color (2016)
Daybed (2018)
Momently (2024)

Prose

Events Film Cannot Withstand (2011)
Diving Makes the Water Deep (2016)

Chapbooks

The Man Who Lost His Head (2011)
The Motherwell Sonnets (2023)

I go looking for lines in Zach Savich's *A Field of Telephones* to synthesize the scope of his project, but finding the right one would boil down to a xerox of the entire text. You do not need to know Theodore Roethke—"a mind made manifold in relation to another"—to become absorbed by his obsession with the word, framed by Savich's gratitude for the beauty of the moment. *A Field of Telephones* makes play of his encounters with this minor-major poet, producing vivid characters that come, go, and recur with the speed of thought itself. Savich, at some point, calls this "happiness."

— Jess Barbagallo

Imagine Theodore Roethke were to prank-call academia from his greenhouse in the sky. Zach Savich would act as the switch to route the call into seer-reviewed criticism. *A Field of Telephones* spirals the lecture form into slapstick, where stage directions are cardinal and Modernism is "the great comic hippo" in the room. A variety act of the personal and the theoretical (*Laughter*), the Midwestern and the cosmic (*Disaster*), glee glitches rhyme into meaning (*Poetaster*), and marginalia takes centerstage (*Ta-da!*). Poetry's circus is here, offering the gift of an error in your ear: "Watch out! I'm talkin' here!" Embracing that hybrid line between experimental and experiential, Savich~~'s speaker~~ desires a clocktime measured in "moments," one that goes ping-pong instead of tick-tock, one where we stop and smell the telephones, the cellular, the satellite. If we are to "spend" life on poetry, what does its cha-ching bring, really? Pick this up. Experiment the moment. Answerve.

— Henry Goldkamp, author of *Joy Buzzer: A Clown Show*

If a telephone rings and no one hears, did a tree fall in the same shaggy dog story twice? *A Field of Telephones* is a book of rhymes and counter-rhymes, criticism and closet drama, all teetering in the same trench coat. Every action has a chain reaction: "A triggering town," for Savich, triggers "a brigadier clown, a Frigidaire swan." There's no there there, there's no air air, here's an aye aye for an eye, highway robbery. Adjunct firefighters have well-endowed poles. This is a mind-bendingly tender lecture (plus Q&A) on Theodore Roethke, with a break for coffee and synonym bums between the poetic feet (literally—the phones and phonemes are shoes. All soles rejoice!). "Poetry is mostly tone…a dial tone…pretending to be speech…" I can't help but hear Charles Bernstein, reciting the yellow pages: "Fence. Fence. Fence." *A Field of Telephones* also isn't not a book about cancer. Tumors rear their heads, recede, rears, recede. Yet the form itself is cancerous, but in a benign sense: sounds multiplying into ideas, associations riffing into references, alliterations ballooning. It's "pure pun-logic, pier pin Legos, pour pine Legolas, a pioneer pineal jig." If this is hold music, play on.

— Adrienne Raphel, author of *Our Dark Academia*

Zach Savich's prose wears the mark of the poet's charge: to direct attention, to engender curiosity, to chronicle insight, and to suspend time.

— Full Stop

[Savich's] prose invites the reader to perform mental gymnastics, the twists of which keep orbiting in the mind after the book is closed…Sits among the high-water marks for the impact that nonlinear, lyrical memoir is capable of.

— Diagram

A FIELD OF TELEPHONES

Zach Savich

53rd State Press
Brooklyn, NY

March 2025
Brooklyn, NY

A Field of Telephones
© Zach Savich 2025
53rdstatepress.org

ISBN Number: 979-8986581477
Library of Congress Control Number: 2024951121

Book design: Kate Kremer
Cover design: w/d

Printed on recycled paper in the United States of America.

All rights reserved. Except for brief passages quoted in reviews, features, or essays, no part of this book may be reproduced without permission in writing from the publisher. This material, being fully protected under the Copyright Laws of the United States of America and all other countries of the Berne and Universal Copyright Conventions, is subject to a royalty. All rights, including but not limited to professional, amateur, recording, motion picture, recitation, lecturing, public reading, radio and television broadcasting, and the rights of translation into a foreign language, are expressly reserved. Particular emphasis is placed on the question of readings and all uses of this book by educational institutions, permission for which must be secured from the author.

A Field of Telephones is made possible by the New York State Council on the Arts with the support of the Office of the Governor and the New York State Legislature.

"I have said uncharitable things, even in my sleep, about every new critic that ever wrote."
—Theodore Roethke

"I think I know enough to know."
—The Halo Benders

CONTENTS

A Field of Telephones..13

Hugo Scenes, 1–5..25

First Lecture..41

Hugo Scenes, 6–8..65

The Wild Kindness..77

Hugo Scene, 9...83

Second Lecture...85

Caryl's Lecture..107

Hugo Scenes, 10–12..117

What Book...127

Hugo Scene, 13...137

Third Lecture...141

Hugo Scenes, 14–18..155

Acknowledgments...173

Selected Sources..175

Contributors..177

[Setting:

Begin at a bus stop outside of the old Richard Hugo House in Seattle, recreated in Cleveland.

Start to read. The bus is late. Walk to the next bus stop. Read some more.

Walk to the next bus stop. The bus is late. Read some more.]

A FIELD OF TELEPHONES

The new friend asks me to tell her something about myself that she doesn't know. I was never a kid who could say their favorite color. I liked colors. I told the teacher I wasn't sure when blue became green. She had me tested for color blindness. Once, I misread *birding* as *braiding*. The branches wove.

. . .

I hadn't been asked a question like that in a minute. There's the idea that your life story starts when something happens that you'd need to mention before you could say anything else. There's the other idea that your life story starts after the above has passed and you could start your story anywhere. I'm interested in the story after and around the story we "need to tell."

. . .

Jack Gilbert: "What I'm interested in is writing about people who have gotten beyond the beginning." (Yet also: we ask of each sentence, could this be, at last, our final, eventual beginning, however late or untoward?)

. . .

Or: I don't need to tell you where I've been, for us to be here, but we can talk if you want.

. . .

I said I was working on a study of the poet Theodore Roethke (1908–1963). I was about to go to Saginaw, Michigan, his hometown. Isn't there a song about Saginaw, the other new friend said. Lefty Frizzell's "Saginaw, Michigan." 1964. We were waiting on the pretzel bites. She began to sing: "I was born in Saginaw, Michigan. I grew up in a house on Saginaw Bay."

. . .

For a long time the story I needed to tell before saying anything else was cancer. My thirties. I often didn't need to tell it. It was obvious. I got used to people in public asking if I was all right. The palliative doctor asked what I wanted. "Moments," I said.

. . .

The person who says they want "moments" knows they may have only "moments" left. Sun on my wrist one afternoon I could handle it, among treatments. I preferred the light when it steadily flared.

. . .

I was born a bit southeast of Saginaw. The house was sunflowers taller than anyone. I saw a stranger peeing in the raspberries.

. . .

Sun tea on a stone. Potato bugs under.

. . .

Johnny Cash covers Frizzell's song. A mix of hardscrabble and schmaltz: very Roethke. Consider the beginning of his poem "The Saginaw Song":

> *In Saginaw, in Saginaw,*
> *The wind blows up your feet,*
> *When the ladies' guild puts on a feed,*
> *There's beans on every plate*

. . .

The palliative doctor was a few years ago. The few-years-ago tumor was in a scar from an earlier tumor, or was in the scar from a tumor from before that. It felt a little obvious, redundant. "You can't punch yourself in the same tumor twice," a friend said.

. . .

The rhymes above are slick. Neither "feed" nor "plate"

rhymes with "feet," not exactly. But each picks up part of the sound. Their chime with "feet," therefore, is more ambient. An overtone that emerges from plucking the string of "feed" and the string of "plate." The rhyme with "feet" isn't a single harmony, it's a harmonic.

. . .

The harmonic, which emerges within and exceeds.

. . .

Rhyme is not a matching game. It arranges, activates, assembles. And, in the next two lines, it shifts, settles: "And if you eat more than you should, / Destruction is complete." We end with a resolution, "complete" calling back to "feet," fulfilling the ambient effect generated by "feet / feed / plate." Resolving the imperfect matching. Meanwhile, "should," in calling back to the "d" in "feed," establishes a counterchord, an undertone, with dissonance: "complete / feed" echoing through "feet / feed / should." Rhyme is in motion. Ambient, acute.

. . .

Forms of language are forms of thought, as we often said. Ways of swimming. You don't need to use them, but you'll use them, in ways, in particular waters. And everyone who used them, who really used them, or who I want to say really used them, really needed to swim. There's no language without it, just as there's no swimming without the body. Even in stillness, the body is moving. In the silentest reading. You can't move any part without moving everywhere. Reeds in the shallows and mixing the colder depths and the warm algae.

. . .

"I don't want you to have to find my body," I said to my wife, during those years of moments. "I can find your body," she said.

. . .

Hardscrabble, schmaltz: this was the landscape, childhood. In Saginaw, Roethke receives a postcard from his cousin, in 1916. It shows a macaroni factory ("last year Larkin customers received more than 1,000,000 packages of macaroni"). "Dear Theodore," the message reads. "We are just going through this factory. It is very large."

. . .

Another, from the cousin on a visit to Detroit, sweetly: "Hello Theodore. How do you feel after your picnic?" And here's one from his father, in 1918, a few years before the father's death. "We are all having a good time and I shot a deer the first day in the woods be a good boy and help Mama all you can Papa."

. . .

The father's death defined his life. He didn't return to Saginaw when his mother was dying.

. . .

A landscape, childhood. His father's greenhouses, 25 acres. Up in the night to fiddle the steam. Visible from his bedroom window, immortal diamond. "It was a jungle, and it was paradise," he wrote. In the present, shards of glass sometimes work their way up in neighbors' gardens.

. . .

Shards of glass working their moments up in neighbors' gardens. This is the legacy, a university.

. . .

Father and uncle ran the business. Largest florist in Michigan. Manure and roses. Lived next door to it and each other. Then the business went bad and the uncle killed himself and the father died from cancer and the poet wore a long black coat for years. "Carnations, verbenas, cosmos."

. . .

Our garden was a little strip. Even the smallest strip can be a garden. Fecund glitch. From my bedroom, I could see the tree with snowball blossoms. Put one down your pants. Bare room, wood. Light I have seen a few times since.

. . .

I asked my friend the attorney, "What advice would you give me for finding an attorney, in case it helps with dying?" "My advice is, I will be your attorney," he said.

. . .

I asked the friend who lived in a state where some laws might help with dying about establishing residency in their state. "You officially live with me now," they said.

. . .

Or there was the friend who asked if it'd be easier to know, if it came to it, that he'd take care of my clothes. Nothing to worry about.

. . .

In the archives at the University of Washington, in Seattle, among the postcards and other items of Roethke's childhood, there's a set of collectible cards that recall the more saccharine, jaunty moments from his poems, especially in his lighter pieces and poems for children. One shows a dopey, grinning kid whittling near a windmill. "De happiness off my heart sprouts oudt off my face," it says. Another shows a boy and a dog: "If I had viskers like dis feller's I vunder vould I be somebody's pet." Another: "The moon in the sky is a custard pie."

. . .

"I had a Donkey, that was all right, / But he always wanted to fly my Kite," begins his poem, "The Donkey." Sensibility oh la.

. . .

I surrendered my pens, sanitized my hands. I told the librarian that I was a scholar of materiality who interpreted biographical effects, authors' notebooks, and other physical ephemera as sculptural artifacts. I needed to touch the stuff, bypass the microfiche. So held a lock of his childhood hair up to my ear. "Theodore's first haircut."

. . .

After which my notes digressed into a shaggy meditation on Keats' poem about a lock of Milton's hair. Cut it.

. . .

And put on his glasses. Opened the cigarette case that had been in his pocket when he died, swimming in a pool outside Seattle. Counted the cigarettes in it, strained for a lyrical thought: *These would have become his breath*. Blew a small whistle. Keys he stole from hotels.

. . .

Is heritage lineage? Or an echoing wood, "a steady stream of correspondences." This shaking that speaks through us. In which meaning is. Or in which meaning is released.

. . .

The librarian, interested that I was a poet, told me he'd been friendly with Elizabeth Bishop when she briefly taught there, shortly after Roethke's death. They once went for a drive. She said a field of flowers looked like a field of telephones.

[Setting:

The first "Hugo Scenes" (1–12) are best to imagine in a high school gym, after hours. Who ordered this assembly? Or in a rural theatre, near a sawmill.

The action can be implied.]

HUGO SCENE, 1

the ventriloquist requests a volunteer…

no, no: he insists…you in the front…let's see what you have to say for yourself…what's your name…

Brad…let's hear it for Brad…

now Brad put this on…yes the straps and…you can still see his eyes folks but what can his eyes see…the less the better he'll probably be thinking…

the nose over the nose…cheeks over his cheeks…

I'd say you're looking pretty presidential Brad… maybe even professorial…

(*strokes* BRAD's *head*)…I've always thought education should be about making energy intellectual…that's different from making intellectuality intellectual…

and yes the mouth over the mouth…dangling…it talks when I pump it like this…

how ya feeling Brad…

>   (BRAD *voice, ventriloquized, the mouth of the mask flapping as the ventriloquist talks for* BRAD *and pumps*) at last I can live like a human…

what were you before…

(BRAD *voice, deflatingly but also a little to-be-so-bold*) I couldn't say…

HUGO SCENE, 2

it's good to "find" "your" "voice" isn't it folks...
but better when your voice finds you...finds you
with your pants down maybe but there you are...a
real butt...

oh Brad and by the way...that embarrassing thing
you ordered in the mail...which you thought might
help you at last be the real you...you accidentally
entered the address of every other house in the
city...they hate you now...what can I say...we live
among compensatory damages...

now Ronnie will sing the national anthem in the
lasers...you should remember him from *Vanilla
Sky*...these are his real teeth...

tell us about *Vanilla Sky*, Brad...

> (BRAD *voice*) if I do can I have a kiss

>> (VENTRILOQUIST *pumps mask so
>> the mouth puckers, suckles*)

ha ha any takers out there...I'd be careful though
because...

> (BRAD *voice*) what you don't think I'm pretty...

now Brad why would you...you've never looked
better...but just so you and more importantly

everyone else understands...that mask is electrified for things like

>(*puts a hog dog in the puckered, suckling mouth, until it's on fire, puts it in* BRAD's *shirt pocket like a cigar for a new dad*)

and also so that...well, try to pull it off Brad...

>(*a zap, nose spins, jazz hands*)

(BRAD *voice*) well, that wasn't all bad...

what do you mean...

>(BRAD *voice*) I don't have to pee anymore...

HUGO SCENE, 3

this is our critical pageant…a variety show…little scummy…starting any minute now…consider the mask Brad's fellowship…a real honor…

our subject tonight is Richard Hugo's *The Triggering Town*…our title is "The Triggering Town: Richard Hugo's *The Triggering Town* at Forty"…snappy right…

forty refers to me…I'm about to turn…the book's a little older, a classic…if forty is old enough for that…I read it first…who cares when…I lived in towns he knew…the wind bled coupons into earth…and the milk ran out with the spoon…Aberdeen, La Push…

it's just that easy folks…poetry is mostly tone…a dial tone…pretending to be speech…like how you used to be able to record payphones…certain tones…and there was this one sequence you could record then hold up to the copy machines at Kinko's…a hack…boop boop beep beep beep boop…and then print your zine for free…

I chaperoned the prom…I bought asparagus in the rain…this is Methodist and there is no air…art is what keeps you…I won't say whole…art is what keeps you…perishable…and the trout ran out…it's all right to applaud...

our sponsor tonight is the new university run by firefighters...mostly calendars...safe for work...they're great...they have this new firesuit we'll be showing off tonight...it's not just for firefighters...little girl, would you like one...

the new firesuit also helps when we need Brad to go to sleep...do you all think Brad would like to go to sleep...

AUDIENCE: NAP! THAT! BRAD!

OK Brad get ready...here comes the firesuit...

> (*pale blue sheet put over* BRAD, *mouth pucker/suckle effect comedically visible through the sheet, cartoon snoring sounds,* BRAD *acting like a parrot being put to sleep, a sheet over its cage, which counteracts any more sinister associations though not enough*)

speaking of turning forty...you know that poem by Donald Justice, "Men at Forty"...you know it, don't you Brad...

> (BRAD *wakes, suckles/puckers mouth until sheet chomps off*)

> (BRAD *voice, reciting*) *Men at forty*

Learn to close softly
The doors to rooms they will not be
Coming back to

is it just me or is the changing understanding of great literature over the course of one's life absolutely amazing…a round of applause…I guess my philosophy is you run until you feel the leash and then you hope your head is smaller than your neck…slip through…that's why we need to be careful about learning…hey, Brad…do you ever wonder if it's easier to make your head smaller or your neck larger…

 (BRAD *voice*) why not both…

do you ever feel like you're at the end of your rope…

 (BRAD *voice*) think how the rope feels…

HUGO SCENE, 4

Hugo studied with Theodore Roethke..."probably the best poetry-writing teacher ever," he said...Roethke, a real dancing bear...so there are generations here...a game of telephone...and as Hugo says in *The Triggering Town*...it was easier to shake Roethke's influence as a poet than as a teacher...ventriloquism kind of thing...

> (BRAD *voice, remembering when he tried to remove the mask*) I think it's even easier to shake in general...

that's right, Brad..."this shaking keeps me steady," as Roethke said...but really I guess my philosophy is...you push the critical thing until you can't push it any further...and that's where you build a church around it...like any critical illness...what used to be called tenure...

I hear they have some new endowed poles at the firefighters' university...

oh I heard some professors in the audience are taking exception...they're cute aren't they... they've mobilized to very slowly write a collective statement...oh they're debating the phrasing!... they're referring to their time in graduate school!... someone just brought up a time they wrote a collective statement two decades ago...

meanwhile the university just invented and completed a process that will replace all classes with vending machine malfunction call center help lines...they assure us they'll follow best practices for equitable vending machine malfunction call center help line operations and work-work-work balance...they want to be transparent about that...

the firefighter university president just assured me... it will be inclusive...like adjuncting...

in the meantime Brad and the other Brads will start their game called Dance Marathon...tell me if the dancing slows...just point the laser pointers...yes like that...yes in my eyes...yes more in my eyes... more in my eyes...more in my eyes...that's how I'll know to look...it's important for the performance to never become theatre...

> (BRAD *voice*) you know when I was asleep just then...I had the nicest dream...

what did you dream Brad...

> (*removes a speck from* BRAD*'s mask*)

(BRAD *voice*) can I have a kiss...

> (*another hot dog in the pucker/ suckle, cooks, puts it in* BRAD*'s*

> *pocket, this repeats as much as you like)*

(BRAD *voice*) yum…so in my dream we were all here…but I had the nicest thing…

what was that Brad…

(BRAD *voice*) I had some volunteers of my own…come on up everyone…

> (VOLUNTEERS *join or maybe start to then don't, or point to others in the crowd who they think should volunteer, outfitted variously with masks and/or wearing an array of pale blue sheets/firesuits, leashes, etc., or one gets the sheet put around their neck like at the barber, and* BRAD *starts to chomp/suckle their hair, etc., and someone else holds up the back of someone else's sheet like a wedding dress train, etc., their names are Vic Medici, Candy Koski, Joyce Bebar Cuddles Clueride, Rick Petrov who is a damn fine detective and writes poetry in his free time, Lee and Lynn Hammer, Stinky Rasmussen, Betty Huff, Marge Appleton, Dale*

> *Robbins, Marnie, and Robin Tingley, or any combination)*

now please welcome back Ronnie to sing "Desperado" by The Eagles in his thick voice...we love cover songs don't we folks...don't you think it's best to be among the re-released...

> (BRAD *voice*) does a bear shit in the woods...does the pope shit in his hat...

HUGO SCENE, 5

Hugo's problem, I think, in *The Triggering Town*, is he's trying to explain...should I stop there...

(BRAD *nods bigly*)

Hugo's problem is he's trying to explain...period...

Hugo's problem is he's trying to explain a feeling he must have felt enough to feel he should explain it...but having felt it so much he knows...he can't... that is, why'd he spend his life on poems...what's wrong with him...what was he hoping for...why'd he feel like that was the best or only thing to do... and to keep doing...he doesn't know why...his explaining doesn't get it...he knows that...so why is he trying...I don't think birds particularly *like* their nests...they just live there...they make them... it's no critique of the nest if...the bird doesn't like it and...it fits the bird...

like Hugo says...a writer can feel bad when they're not writing...so then they think whenever they feel bad...it's from not writing...here's a drug that can cause madness or...if you are currently mad... cures it...

his title's "triggering" isn't triggering in the contemporary sense...like a trigger warning...he means things that catalyze, inspire…for him, a "small town that has seen better days often works"…but anything can do…"our triggering subjects, like our words, come from obsessions we must submit to"… and I thought poets mostly submitted to magazines…

yet Hugo seems to mean most…he's talking about any subject seen *as though* it's a town…move around your subject, he says…see who's up…you can show them around…you could have any triggering subject, as he says…but he's also asking you to look at any subject like it's a town…a locus of lives, real or imagined or our own…a triggering town, a brigadier clown, a Frigidaire swan…therefore, and this is the real critical thing…however private he claims his poems are, ideally, their craft's a civic vision…you can find plenty of essays about it I'm sure…

tourists in a non-tourist spot…Hawthorne's "Wakefield"…Whitman after manifest destiny has passed him by…cohesive regionalism of the defunct…loading docks…Panera now has fried chicken and cheap pizza and there's this hack where you put the hashbrowns from McDonald's and the fish from Wendy's on the pizza from Panera…Tom Petty on every station…the team apparel just shows us what was in the donation box…the accent is dental…two hot dogs for a dollar no matter what you might be about to do…say what you will…

[Setting:

The three Roethke lectures took place in July, 2023, at the Theodore Roethke House in Saginaw, Michigan, kinda.

Gracious thanks to the Friends of Theodore Roethke!]

FIRST LECTURE

It's hard to imagine a better setting for a week of lectures about Theodore Roethke. Can you hear me? "Roethke viewed the self as continually seeking a harmonious dialogue with all that is," as Ralph J. Mills wrote. So that's what we'll go for tonight. Thanks to Betty Huff for adjusting the lights so that—when I turn like this—see, there's Roethke's profile. My hair is his nose, its shadow, and the clock on the mantle is his brow. The lectern's his gut. Someone asked if I had an outline for the evening's talk—there it is. That silhouette's my outline. A full-body suit kinda shadow. What did they say his favorite meal was? Porterhouse steak, and a deep-dish martini.

(*Laughter*)

I know what you're thinking. Anyone who'd be interested in a week of lectures about Theodore Roethke might be interested *no matter what* the setting is, but this one—living room of his childhood home—is pretty special. I love those fireplace tiles. I heard they found them in the attic a while ago. There's that thought from André Breton, who you are is who you haunt. Roethke's haunting us, as we haunt the place. Don't think I won't answer that antique phone and listen for him if it rings. I'll tell him all my secrets until he talks.

I want to start with the question of legacy, the present.

Why Roethke, why now. As the mountain climber said, breathing out, "Because it was *air*." Well, Roethke did write: "Loving, I use the air most lovingly. I breathe." I wouldn't mind being used like that. That line actually takes us to his student, Richard Hugo, following the drift of the word "air"—our game of telephone, this field of telephones. There's that film of Hugo teaching, when he's live-revising a student's poem, and he focuses on this one line: "This is Methodist and there is no air." The line is buried a bit in the student's poem. But that's the real start, he says. The engine turns over. The turnovers are delicious. The students are what you'd probably call co-eds, smoking cigarettes in class, Montana, the '70s. I used to show that clip as a way to talk about what we wouldn't do in a poetry workshop—mostly, we wouldn't just have me go on and on about what their poems were actually about. Though the moment is interesting in a scholarly sense, or in the senses I prefer to call scholarly, because that line Hugo says is the real start? It sounds like a sound he was often listening toward, in his own poems. "This is Methodist and there is no air" sounds a lot like a line of his like, for example, "but that is auditory and will not do." Can you hear that? A harmonic, ringing through. The real start, whenever it happens, should startle us.

Anyway, it's a particular honor to think about legacy in this setting. "We must permit poetry to extend consciousness as far, as deeply, as particularly it can," Roethke wrote. I mean "particular" in that sense—what can poetry and thinking about poetry particularly *do*? We see a lot happening with the fate of the humanities, the contemporary university. Questions of survival. Leveraging strategic utility. It can be pretty different from the fantasy we might have had about the university, about learning and the public good. But this site, what they've made of his childhood home, does so much for the public good. Legacy, here, is about more than preserving a reputation, a critical shrine. It's about—all their work with kids, public health, mental health. Roethke suffered in those terms. But the terms were different then. They say his parents used to put up signs for whoever needed it, saying you could get a meal here. We all gather now in that spirit.

"Loving, I use the air most lovingly. I breathe," he said. So, let's err on the side of air, in these talks. What Stein said about Sacramento—"there's no there there"—might be better, especially for Stein's poetics, as "there's no air air." A step away from "aye aye." "The highest minds of the world have never ceased to explore double meanings," as Emerson said, at least twice. Who's he calling high? Roethke would agree, said a poet's "someone who is never satisfied with saying one thing at a time." As if you ever could.

But speaking of double meanings, Roethke does say in one poem: "Light airs! Light airs!" We'll talk about his repetitions later. "Most poets have only a handful of ideas; the best, it seems, have fewer," Luke Brekke wrote. Roethke showed how few ideas he had by repeating them? Maybe. He had "a minimum of 'ideas,' a maximum of 'intuitions,'" as Kenneth Burke said. Anyway, in "Light airs! Light airs!" you'd be right to hear "airs" as "errors," maybe, but it's better to hear "light airs" as an elemental compound. "Airs" comes through initially as a noun, in my doubled hearing, I do have two ears after all, two "errors"—that is, we might hear "light airs" as a reference to the airs that are light. And then we'll hear its secondary register, as a verb. Light airs itself out. But air is complicated, just ask a lung. Especially for a poet with Roethke's relationship to gusts: somewhere he says he "scratched the wind with a stick," a wind that "sharpened itself on a rock." Careful you don't cut yourself on that wind. So, he's in the air, is all I mean, especially here, and it's a very particular air. It's made of piano scales and exhaust from Gratiot Avenue and residues of cosmic junk, an old laceless shoe along the road, quasads or—

AUDIENCE: Quasi-stars.

Something like that. "Was it dust I was kissing," he says somewhere. Which some critics have said is about a dusty mummy or something, a ghost, but I think it's right to hear it as a beam of dust in kitchen light. Right at child-level. Give it a kiss. And remember kissing, for Roethke, is often about creating complex circuits that surge and then burst, from solitary to something solitary-and-something-else: "My lips pressed upon stone," "My own tongue kissed / My lips awake." "Is circularity such a shame?" he asks. I know there are a lot of actual scholars here tonight and many more watching from home (*makes tight-frame thumbs up gestures and waves for the camera*) who know a lot more about this, but, anyway, I'll start off tonight blowing some kisses toward the question of Roethke's legacy. At the time of his death, the question of his legacy being a question might've surprised some people. He'd won all the awards, been one of *the* teachers of his day. Lauded as "the father of the next generation of poets," for his roving engagement with "deep imagery, confessionalism, neo-surrealism, and the return to a kind of pastoral ecstasy" end-quote.

AUDIENCE*:* Who's that from?

I can share notes later. Anyway, that variety has made him hard to pigeonhole, but it's partly why he was such a good poet for me to encounter early, in my own college sweaters. I mean, I was pretty sweaty. He's an anthology. You can open to any page, see something else. That "next generation" that he's the "father" of is commonly thought to mean his students—Hugo, of course, and James Wright, Carolyn Kizer, Tess Gallagher, David Wagoner—but it goes further. Tomorrow night I'll focus on that. And also on where his legacy doesn't go. That is, it really doesn't go to the kind of prosaic, epiphanic free verse tiny-tidy narrative monologue essayistic dioramas popularized in the 1980s as a backlash against modernism, a bulwark against postmodernism. A mode of poetry that is still, sadly, often assumed or insisted on as a kind of normative neutral centrist position in a lot of poetry circles. Sad little skits of wisdom, highlighting the poet's sensitive sensibility and special knowledge. A view of poetry that leaves out most of poetry, let alone people. So many views of poetry leave out most of poetry, let alone people. Those poems should let people alone even more. You know the kind of poem I mean. There's a grabby first line, a theme the speaker worries, with aching control. Vamping through tone. Look at me. They're a little sad, a little suburban, a little knowing. Deep thoughts about Vermeer and weather and a figure from pop culture, whose work is usually more interesting than the poem, maybe jazz. The snacks of childhood. Sticky table after school. A stickiness that's pretty different from the diaphanous lacquers in Roethke, what Burke called "the curative element of primeval slime." Then there's a conclusion that rings like truth, but it isn't anything you wouldn't know already, tiredly. "School of Quietude," some used to call it. Ron Silliman, mostly, in his blog, talking about the "School of Quietude." A school marked by its denial of being a school. Wanting to be the "unmarked case," exempt from aesthetics. Poems that might take as their subject, as William Matthews said, experiences like, "I went out into the woods today, and it made me feel, you know, sort of religious." I prefer "quietus" to "quietude." Quietus speaks of death. Like we have some friends in Cleveland who have this neighbor who throws rotting vegetables over the fence, cans of beans, stale bread, sometimes like half a leftover casserole, little wads of foil? It's something the church has them do, a good deed. That's quietus. Well, it could be, it could be about death, especially if you ate all those casseroles, warm from the grass. An aesthetics not of wallpaper, but of things coming over the fence, more like William Morris when—

AUDIENCE: Brad, is that the same William Morris as the agency?

I don't think so. "Ask the mole," as Roethke said. I mean the artist, designer. Textiles. Poet, too. 19th century. Maybe you mean William Morrow? That's a literary agency, right?

AUDIENCE: No, William Morris, the agency. Here in town. Is that who you mean? I think it was also the 19th century, or close enough. Let me look. (*Spends time with phone.*) Yes. It started in 1898, in Hollywood—

Well, it's all just one step away. Things thrown over the fence. Words for the wind. All my friends and I used to go by the name Ed Bedford. Every word rhymes, when your ears are plugged right. Anyway, Matthews says these poems sound like, "I went out into the woods today, and it made me feel, you know, sort of religious." But Roethke's feelings were far from "sort of." His interiority was loud. Roar if you want. But because of his affiliation with an official verse culture of his day, and his desire to be a tennis star, then a coach, and to get acclaim from those who labor as maître d's at the table of the greatly great, critics who obsessed over whether or not Roethke was, say, the "strongest survivor" of the "middle generation of American poets"—because of all that, he's probably more often thought of alongside poets like Robert Lowell and Richard Wilbur than with the experimental movements that, as I'll get into in a bit, his work is actually closer to. Never mind what a useless phrase "experimental" is. I'm with Stevens: all poetry is experimental, though I'm mostly with myself—it'd be better if we just said *experiential*. A poem either offers a real experience of experience or it doesn't. That's basically what Rukeyser says. We know what we mean by *real*. Or it will show us, in time. The real poem becomes true. Or did.

Like I said, good to see so many actual Roethke scholars here tonight. The doors are locked, I'm sorry. If there's a gas leak or something it will be a great loss to the future of conversations about, you know, the ending of "My Papa's Waltz." Its interpretation on your breath... could make a young boy dizzy. Of course, the point of that poem isn't a New Critical standardized test close reading of how the poem can present itself to multiple readings, and think about dads. The point is it's a waltz. And, this should give us chills in our critical chops, it happened right there, by that piano. That's the point. The right there. The piano. The floor. Step on it. Hear it.

The right there. That's the point of the poem. Right here. But Roethke's closeness to other traditions, to experiment, isn't just about my reading. It's also historical. For example, in 1964, the year his posthumous collection *The Far Field* was published, a reader could also find first editions of Ted Berrigan's *The Sonnets*, John Berryman's *77 Dream Songs*, Denise Levertov's *O Taste and See*, Robert Duncan's *Roots and Branches*, Frank O'Hara's *Lunch Poems*, Amiri Baraka's *The Dead Lecturer*, and many others. An astonishing year. If Perloff and others have sometimes focused on 1955 or '56 as the watershed exemplar in certain strands of US poetry—because of *Howl* and whatnot—1964 might be the year that the fountain burst its jets and surged into the slosh and storms and standing mosquito waters and untraceable streams thrashing and eddying in the above-ground basements of a lot of poetry we know and love today. And thank god for it. I don't mean it was a direct line. But a buzz in the wires. A party line—not like walking a party line, but like picking up the phone and there's the chorus. You could talk about Roethke's work in relation to any of those books. More easily, I think, than you could talk about, say, Berryman's in the same way. Though Berryman's vocal and semantic ranges within individual poems and lines is probably greater. And you have to ignore a lot, if you want to connect Roethke's poetry to Lowell's but not to Levertov's. The links to Duncan—the mysticism, poetic sequences, West Coast vibe—they all seem especially under-lunked. That's what

I say for "under-spelunked." We might need more than a week of lectures. Load up on whatever mush comes over the fence. Can anyone tell me what bears' caves smell like, in winter? That's something Roethke once asked someone he was dating to look into. Look into the caves. She was a librarian.

Now's probably a good time for a break. Any questions or thoughts so far? Things that are standing out to you? Things I'm getting wrong? I like to ask three questions at once, because then you can answer any of them, or just say whatever you want. "The next step beyond must be either silence or gibberish," as Kunitz said about Roethke's work.

AUDIENCE: Brad, I want to make sure I understand what you're suggesting. I'm worried you're erasing a good deal of particularity. Both from the life and the work. Roethke worked hard to absorb and learn from other styles. He made his own style from that process, and he kept it in motion, as you noted. But it was *his*. He prided himself on "doing" Yeats better than Yeats, for example. He wasn't just derivative, as people sometimes said. He derived a lot from others, but that's a good thing. But he wasn't just on the elevator, as it were, with all these other poets, in the same mire—

Right, right. I mean, on one hand, "the image of the mire is usually felicitous," as Burke says. But I'm not saying he was just a composite, some soup of the different, you know, airs of the era. His particularity was too particular for that. He couldn't avoid it. It's like when a poet friend is interviewing for a job-job, and they ask if they should wear a suit, or if that would betray their poetic soul. And I'm like, "You can't hide what a weirdo you are, at least comb your hair, you know. Carry a manila folder. It doesn't have to have anything in it, but make the effort." And then they're like, "OK, I hear you. I'll wear a suit." And they show up in an astronaut suit.

(*Laughter*)

AUDIENCE: But it might be the same voice just putting on masks. How do you know which voice is which? What happens when the sources disappear?

Well, it gets ghostly, probably. And then the question is how can we help the ghosts live differently, through our own action, in our own imperiled lives. "The self's goal is to come into the presence of the multifarious beings and rhythms of its necessary context," as Bernard Quetchenbach said about Roethke. "The soul's potential," he said, involves "discovering the depths of its entanglement." I think Roethke's conscious relationship to others is like that, and so is his relationship to "good form," "good standing," in all the senses. "If the dead can come to our aid in a quest for identity, so can the living—and I mean *all* living things," he wrote. I mean, he's probably the most famous advocate, at least in his time, for imitation, writing "like somebody else." Which, with the "zoopoetical" bent of ecocritics like Aaron M. Moe in mind, can include "somebody elses" that are minnow, snails, a pike. Orchids. Are orchids animals? And doing that can isolate muscles, stretch your range, ventriloquize, which then comes back to your "own" style. To what you can't escape. You find your voice, which is different, which is voices. But think about it. Imagine Roethke doing an imitation exercise along with his class. And they turn in the poems anonymously, try to guess whose is whose. It would've been obvious, I think, which one was his. But he wouldn't realize it. He'd think he'd given himself away through local diction or something. Mentioning a plant. Salal. But he couldn't *not* give himself away. That's true of all of us. Like in that film when Hugo praises that line that sounds like his own line, "This is Methodist and there is no air." There's that air again. It's a little drafty in here, huh? It's almost a universal truth that people teaching writing are often like—I think Frost says somewhere that a poet is like someone who's leaning so completely in one direction, they have to insist they're leaning in the other direction, just so they don't fall over.

(*Laughter*)

Self-deception can be key. I think of a teacher I had whose work held together by the barest, most impossible, delicate leaps. In class, he praised coherence. Narrative, argument, continuity. He must have had always been telling himself to think of coherence at 200%, when writing, just to get his own poems to cohere at a perfect 7% solution. So, that's the conscious side. But I'm thinking of Roethke's work more as a reader, one who finds it. It finds me. And then I have a body. Wind on my face, so I have a face. A different face. A wind-face. Spin to find where you are. Leap to find the earth. Spinning and caught, spinning and caught. "The human problem is to find out what one really *is*: whether one exists, whether existence is possible," as Roethke said.

AUDIENCE: Yes, but in terms of ideology. Or lineage. You mentioned Duncan. He was obviously responding to some very different conditions.

I don't know, is the response itself that different? I mean, I know it's absurd to insist it's interesting that a couple of pretty canonical, famous-in-their-day-and-ours white male poets writing around the same time had some things in common. But lineage, to me, as a poet—it's about the "age of one's line." Carbon-date it. Anyone wanna go on a carbon date with me later? The carbon is mostly air, I think, or the other way around. But if we look at Duncan's book next to Roethke's from that same year, it's clear that Duncan could also be called a progenitor of "deep imagery, confessionalism, neo-surrealism, and the return to a kind of pastoral ecstasy." I just mean that maybe we shouldn't see those styles as separate pigeons each poet variously kicked into the wind but as a swirling flock. Not a means to a wind—those poetic ranges are a wind in themselves. But this is starting to become about me, I know. When I started getting serious about poetry, people loved talking about hybridity. How to borrow from this school and that school, cross-pollinate, make a chimera. "Appropriation" still more often in its cultural studies sense, I think. In terms of the making or expressing of subculture, alternatives. That's what we were trying to do. Very scientific. Or you could sit on the fence. Or you could object to those trends and say that the hybrid, the fence-sitting—it was unconscionable, a way of not taking a position. But it absorbed or co-opted more principled and programmatic poetics. Appropriation in the other sense. Some people said that. But that was part of the same discourse. All of which depended on caring about schools, believing in them. And believing in yourself and others as having knowledge of how this school led to or reacted against some other school. Let's go steal their mascot, let's put their ascots up a flagpole. It was all probably a hangover from the "anthology wars" of the 1960s and all that vestigial talk about "the raw and the cooked," two "competing schools" of poetry. An effect of having teachers who came of age during that. The "raw and cooked" and "competing schools" are phrases from Lowell's National Book Award speech, 1960. But even in that speech he's saying that the poetry he wants takes from both. I used to teach a whole thing about this.

Anyway, looking back—well, I'm not really looking back, because I wasn't there, but I'm looking from here— what strikes me most, in each of those books, is that the poems are more various than my ideas of "Duncan" or "Roethke." Like in Duncan's book, Roethke's 1964 collection includes ditties (Duncan's "Four Songs the Night Nurse Sang," Roethke's "The Chums"), takes on Blake (Duncan's "Variations on Two Dicta of William Blake," Roethke's "Once More, the Round"), primordial romanticism (Duncan's "Strains of Sight," Roethke's "The Shy Man"), and so on. But the resemblance is closest in the metaphysical poems of meditation, sequences like Duncan's "Doves" and Roethke's "The Rose." Roethke's music crackles and fizzes more, the aspirin dissolving cosmic, but where his sound is more subdued, or Duncan's is more heightened, there's nearness. Shall we play a game? Who wrote, "If I think of my element, is it not fire"? Or is the line actually "If I think of my element, it *is* not fire"? Who wrote, "I'd ravel the shroud in a thorn tree / and let the ends hang loose"? Run to that side of the room if you think—

AUDIENCE: Was the second one Roethke?

I forget. But, yes, I suppose the gravel-gasp of "ravel the shroud in a thorn" is telling, but you see what I mean. Anyway, you're right, the sommelier's game of flavors has its limits. They were writing at the same time, with some things in common, coming to us now through contemporary ears. And I should admit, before I'm called to prosodic account, that, deep down, I honestly think every word rhymes, if you say it right, that wasn't a joke, I really do. That is, if it's surrounded by words that activate its latent harmonics in the right matrix. The matrix of the poem that listens harmonically to itself. That's why revising just for coherence often stabs out the stuffing. The real rhymes are spectral, specters from the pulse. A person says a hard thing, another responds—that's a rhyme, or the pulse between the statements is. Pulse, of course, differs from cadence, or rhythm. It's present not just in the speech but after you stop speaking. A particular pulse from each poem.

AUDIENCE: Is this the same as Rilke's angel?

Well, remember Rilke was a big fan of Quaker oats.

(*Laughter*)

But, seriously, it's probably the same pulse, or angel, as in Horace: "nunc est bibendum, nunc pede libero pulsanda tellus." I should've held up my phone and had it say the Latin, moved my lips along. It just means, "Now we ought to drink and knock the earth." That's the pulsa, pulsanda. A knock on the earth. Which is dancing. A waltz. Same earth that Celan said was inside, so we dug. So. My point is just that we can, and thus should, think about Roethke's work more broadly. With wider relevance. And the inability to see this, to instead act like this version or that version of Roethke is most critically true, as so many critics have done, or to set up strawman jousts where, like, Roethke is opposed to Ashbery or something, whatever "Ashbery" means to people who still talk about Ashbery that way—that's a problem.

OK, now's probably a good time for a break? There's coffee and some local birch beer and cinnamon buns. Let a cinnamon bun sit in some birch beer for a while, it might ferment a little, get us a little closer to that martini. I'll meanwhile be over by the fire, working on a joke about "cinnamon buns." By joke I mean a groaning rhyme. Maybe "synonym bums"? That's what poets often are.

. . .

Welcome back. I've been told some folks just joined online. So I'll go back and let's do that first part all over again for them, word for word? I'm kidding. I couldn't anyway. I write down thoughts to move on from thoughts. I say things so I'll never have to say them again. I get lonelier with every word.

What I want to do now is sketch a little syllabus, then we can talk more. Read some poems. The point is always how we might talk after, or how we can talk only when we're talking about poems.

I'll start with another San Francisco Renaissance hero—I wish I had someone who'd bust through the wall, playing the part, all suited up. A volunteer? Step right up. I'll tell you what to say. And then I'll never have to say anything again. I'm thinking of Jack Spicer. He gave some lectures kinda like these once, right before he died, at forty. Were any of you there? Born a bit after Roethke, died a couple years later. Of that era, and maybe more than most poets I've mentioned so far tonight, he was also of ours? Question mark. An eternal ours, a brook of ours, eternal in the sense that "eternal" always means mostly how we imagine the eternal, from here. Chatty O'Hara can seem stilted next to him, is what I mean. Spicer's poems could be in most of the most interesting magazines today. Like Roethke, he also defied the truism that good poets are easy to parody, difficult to imitate. That's often true, I guess. Because, you know, it's easy to imitate a bad poem, but how could you parody it. It's already a parody. But real bangers—you can mock them—"I got hard for us all, my only swerving"—but imitations often clang palely back to the source. All bricks, no caulk or spores or vines. Roethke and Spicer, in contrast, are difficult to parody and difficult to imitate. First, it's because they're often in motion. A moving target. Second, at times they seem to be consciously parodying/imitating themselves. Those two factors work together. The work can seem self-responsive, even self-delighted, even when stricken. And that moves them to move in other directions. As though the motion is: "Was I really pleased by that? I was. But also: ugh. Better do something else…" But they just keep doing the only thing they can—that is, it's all they can do. Give it your all, your tired, poor, huddled all.

I know that Spicer didn't actually care about intentions in that way. He cared about dictations, from the unknown, his Martians. Radio signals. Poetry was just Martian radio signals. Pick it up. It fills the room like furniture we can then arrange, given what we have. That is, given what we "have to say," which can be said with at least three emphases: what we're obliged to say, what we're compelled to say, and then there's the Spicerian sense, of what we have, what we possess. "The wires in the rose are beautiful." And that's basically the view of most poets throughout time, that poetry is coming from somewhere else. It's probably best to just accept that's how things work, if you're a poet, whatever you think you're saying about your work, about poetry. It's coming from yourself, but that self is also something else, even if that something else may as well be thought of as a self? A music. Substitute "culture" for any of those words, if you prefer. My point is that Roethke, I think, cared more about poetry than about a particular fingerprint. Which is exactly what leads to a particular fingerprint. It emerges, through pressing, more whorled and whirling because of its wideness. The thumb is wilder than the eye. Than the aye aye.

Or, as Nicholson Baker wrote in *The Anthologist*, a book that's full of Roethke, "Poetry is a controlled refinement of sobbing." That makes the fingerprint. Sure as a spiral in a cut trunk. For Roethke, one part of that fingerprint is a line of jaunty iambic pentameter that pauses on the seventh syllable, then there's a three-syllable phrase: "Of those so close beside me, which are you?" Or: "I think the dead are tender. Shall we kiss?"

But Roethke's closeness to Spicer might be clearest when

he's at his funniest. I don't mean when he adopts the posture of avuncular wag—the blustery faculty club "wit" that led one of his contemporaries to say that Roethke's "consciously funny topical verses, quips at the audience, topical references, and jokes about others and himself often fell below his best level of private spontaneous humor." Definitely nothing I should learn from that assessment in terms of self-knowledge. And which another described as "second-rate night club comedy." Modes that can feel anxious, insecure, sophomoric and professorially invested in impressing sophomores. And which still pass as wit in some tiresome neo-formalist circles today. College boys, scared of turning forty. Check out Eliot Weinberger's essay about New Formalism, which then veers into a discussion of really elaborate Icelandic formalism, a dare to those who'd plop plop plop their rhythmic nuggets into some sunless mechanical metrical bull. But I'm thinking of the moments in Roethke's poetry that are funny like a funny bone, or a clown who keeps hitting their own. In "The Long Alley," for example, Roethke abruptly declares, "Nuts are money." Those psychosexually obsessed early critics might see those nuts one way. Their currency. They said everything in Roethke was either the phallus or masturbation. Unless it wasn't. In which case it was definitely castration or impotence. And which others might see as regression to a childish economy, or whatever, but I see it literally. Nuts are money. Ask the squirrels. Nuts are money! Chant it like in a gameshow: NUTS! ARE! MONEY!

AUDIENCE: I remember one critic saying whenever he referred to hands, it was jacking off…onanism…

Right, or others said the "head of a match" was masturbation, oh and then—they were getting excited!—the "cat's wish" was the feminine, or something, and "rout the fish" was a release of semen, and the "goat's mouth" was some specter of lecherous mockery? All in one stanza. What a party. But the actual stanza is stranger and more alive. Like sex itself, I suppose, when it's not just a critical system, or when it's an actually critical system. Things might surprise you. "Renew the light, lewd whisper," as Roethke said. Perversity, as Emily Ogden reminds us, can be thinking you know. Cat, fish, goat—I don't know, why not see a barnyard, and even if there's masturbation, the goat is just there, a goat in the barnyard, not a symbol? That's closer to the tradition of the eclogue, its deeper psychology. Or there's the instance I find most annoying, which impacted my reading for years. Roethke writes, "A lively understandable spirit / Once entertained you. / It will come again." I like hearing that "it" as numinous, undefined. That feels most true. And it makes the most sense. "It" is a general reference. A phonebook that has everything's number. But of course the repressed critics saw smut, said they understood that "it" is, like, just the desire for self-pleasure or something—and as though self-pleasure is so limited. As though the self is. Burke, as usual, got it mostly better. He said, "As there is a mind's eye, a spirit breath, an inner ear, so [Roethke] would seem

to conceive of a kind of transcendent sex-within-sex."
That's better than bad Freud.

We just have a few minutes left, so real quick, then we can pick it up tomorrow: the similarity of humor in Spicer and Roethke is about them responding, not just to what a line said, but responding propulsively *past* what it said, to the unsaid and emergent meanings peripheral and echoing throughout. It's like any peripheral zone you move into and then, standing there, you feel the periphery shift. You need to keep moving to keep finding it. Standing among its shifting, by shifting with it. Or it's like pedaling faster than a bike's homeostatic rhythm while racing downhill. That's slapstick: the bike is now riding you. In a Shakespearean sense, we could think of when Hamlet (I'm going on what I've heard) hears an unsaid criticism in a thing he says to himself, then swivels to answer that. To answer to that. "Implication" vs. "implicature" can be a useful critical distinction. As discussed by, for instance, Terence Cave. "Implicature" as an implication that the author intended. Roethke and Spicer are hearing and responding to multiple potential implicatures of their own? I'll think about that more. It can get ecstatic, is my point. Like each struck string tunes the others around it, which then ache to be played, and thus are resounding already in some half-heard but silent chord. It's important to remember that Roethke admired the work of René Char and Henri Michaux.

We'll talk about that more later. Slapstick is also a way to spin the specter. I mean scepter.

HUGO SCENE, 6

welcome back from our latest intermission…which is still happening or about to, it's hard to tell… how's that birch beer float…we make it ourselves… once someone found a wedding ring in one…I had to stop Brad from saying something about "bitch beer" just then…

let's hear it for Ronnie holding that note for the entire intermission…

now while we're waiting for the next bit…and I mean bit like straight from the horse's mouth…we're going to ask Brad to build us a dunk tank without getting wet…Brad…hey, Brad…have you heard about those mythological creatures condemned to carry their own heads around…

    (BRAD *voice*) but that's what we all do…

so he'll build us a dunk tank without getting wet… you'll see he's in the full firesuit now

> (*sheet cinched around* BRAD *with leashes and wires and hoses, a kind of jump suit, like for a failed astronaut*)

don't worry it's a firesuit, he'll be OK…of course it's also still electrified which helps with the whole situation...which is why he shouldn't get wet...

(touches BRAD's *arm kindly)*

don't worry we can control more than just the mouth...but I'm going to need some help to make sure he does what he wants...a whole committee... you'll all control the legs, the arms, the butt with your applause and those lasers...reference to Chris Burden's piece, 1971...people on wooden ladders in electrified water, a duration...Brad's goal in contrast is to construct the dunk tank and move the water into it from this kiddie pool...then he'll tell us about his training...the "areas" he's touched on...I hear he was once a finalist!...

we're gonna turn up the heat in here to make sure time is an interesting concept...if Brad waits too long the water will evaporate and you'll hear this evaporation animation sound effect and game over...it's fun to be impatient isn't it folks...fate is impatient...

some of you were here the other night and the question came up...about how all this connects to Hugo...well first I think the thing to remember might be...influence exceeds its author...like how the influence of *The Triggering Town* helped form all those MFA programs where...you get a car and drive around until...you hit a deer and then you sit by the body until...you realize it's your dad, or the absence of dad...

> (BRAD *voice*) what does the absence of dad have in common with...the dad-sense of abs...easy...love handles...

those cars handled pretty well too...in a cultural sense, after all those early MFA programs graduated their student drivers...each of whom also founded an MFA program...in some programs you all had to share a car...or they just gave the whole cohort one deer...or just some jerky...one part of a car...you've heard about crash-test dummies...these students were *craft*-test dummies...

anyway, I don't think influence is who you'd like to be...it might be who you'd like to please...it's all more familial...though less genetic...

the question of generations...the question is how to restore a sense of the miraculous...outside of a miracle...without the substitute-miraculous being horrific...or bitter...

> (BRAD *voice*) outside of a miracle it's too dark to see...but outside of a duck...it's too *drake* to see...

HUGO SCENE, 7

the "Wakefield" energy in Hugo is, quoting Hawthorne, "he had contrived, or rather he had happened, to dissever himself from the world—to vanish—to give up his place and privileges with living men, without being admitted among the dead. The life of the hermit is nowise parallel to his"...

the dream of showing up somewhere and it's fine but doesn't matter...fried mozzarella, a vanishing point...the sauce is mostly sugar...the sawdust is mostly boogers...you can follow someone and they don't realize it because they're having a more complicated fantasy about being followed...

blending in at the pitiable high school baseball game...seeing two twins on the same team trade jerseys...barber asleep in his chair...he's not really asleep...

I first read "Wakefield" living next door to a missing man...Massachusetts...presumed dead, known locally for construction schemes...silt piles across his property...alarms and trip wires in places you just had to admire...he'd been missing for months... but don't worry...Boy Scouts still put up "Bring Chucky Home" posters...held these hopeful spaghetti suppers...

hope may be cruel…this wasn't hope…but cruel… Chucky wasn't coming home…on one hand, he was dead…on the other, he was any Wakefield's dissipation fantasy…a painless immolation… embodiment of a meaningless clot…inconsequential quiet filibuster the aura of which outlasts your life…

the story of Wakefield, I should've said, is about a man who leaves his wife and lives across the street from her for many years and watches her in her presumed widowhood then one day comes back for dinner…it's OK to applaud…

later that winter, as the fundraisers and search parties continued, my wife and I (she wasn't my wife) strode the old New England asylum grounds… New England is mostly old asylum grounds…

the snow held her…not me…we glazed and crunched our way…we could live like that…we did…but I want to end this part with a vivid memory…

that New Year's Eve, my housemate Joel hurled his wedding ring from the porch then sledded down to it…a Wakefield microcosm…we threw stones and snowballs and a small axe after him…he was our Brad, as we were his…he found the ring in the snow…his marriage would outlast us all…I think the one who threw the axe loved him most…but of course, since it was me, I would say that…

(BRAD *voice*) of course you would, speaking of axes…but also, speaking of axes, *wood* would say whatever it was moved to…hey what did the wood say when it was moved by the axe…"let's split"…what did the axe say in reply…"you *wood*"…

HUGO SCENE, 8

OK so for this dunk tank game Brad's tools are under the inflatable pool…hmm…that's right, Brad, kick them up…kick them from under the inflatable…careful of that water…

OK he found the axe…it got dry from the evaporation heat effect…he's using it on the tree…nice, Brad, nice…

a pile of perfect boards appears in place of the tree…fit them together into dunk tank frame shape…there you go…

he's not sure what to do next…let's help him out…yes the lasers…that's right, the arms, the butt…oh, is he getting discouraged…don't worry, he's still breathing…and he's very well-rested…he slept at intermission in the ballpit…little socks around each ball in the ballpit…that's what he uses for sheets…

hmm…the heat is really evaporating, isn't it…he's thinking there should be plexiglass or something to fill in the dunk tank frame shape…then he could add the water…oh, game over…Brad died of hunger…there's a lot of concern about AI in writing lately but I think writing has always been algorithmically combinatory and is it that different if you get your thesis from a dream or a faculty advisor or a bot…I still haven't seen actual evidence that every word isn't also every other word...the etymology of most words if you go back far enough is "church"...but writing is insisting it matters that one word isn't any other word...or some other word...not for precise meaning...but for meaning that exceeds...the insisting is the meaning...it exceeds...

round 2...fight!...this time he gets the drill...help him use it on the tree...use the applause and the lasers...laser his drill hand...maple syrup pours from the tree...he sops it with his firesuit, suckles...good sopping, Brad...that will keep him from dying from hunger...that's real maple syrup folks...$24.99 in the lobby...

he's thinking there should be glass or something to complete the dunk tank frame shape...uh-oh he's feeling that old hopelessness sink in...a "watery drowse," as Roethke said...he sloshes water from the kiddie pool straight into the dunk tank frame shape, in case it somehow magically stays there...nope...sloshes out...electrocuted...game over animation sound...

OK now I think he's getting it...applaud to help him get it...in some games there's a two-part experience...you play and appreciate how it was made, how gamey...like in a poem that isn't playful to read, not exactly, but you see it was made through some playful approach, or it has a playfulness you can witness, some wit...playing is one thing and thinking about it is another...but in other games, or poems, it's more of a one-part experience...the experience of playing/reading is itself the game... you're in it...like Brad...all poems are experimental meaning experiential...all poems are occasional meaning the occasion is the poem...there you go, he's using the axe on the hill, breaking it down to plain grass...

use axe on grass...schist...use axe on schist... clay...use axe on clay...oops he uncovered a secret tomb..."who stunned the dirt into noise?"...that's a lot of feathers and ghosts isn't it folks...who knew feathers would stick to ghosts like that...don't worry they're made from real hair...game over...

OK he avoided the secret tomb this time...let's give him some encouragement...use axe on clay...sand... put sand in kiddie pool?...you can't fill a dunk tank with mud...game over...

OK I think he's getting it...he's doing his best... he remembers sand can become glass...he's using the mirrors on the inside of his mask and the evaporation heat effect...those mirrors are there for his own protection, don't worry...he knows he's safe, firefighters are on hand, tenured firefighters from the university, which keeps him vigilant... using the mirrors with the evaporation heat effect...

if he can get the angle right, let's help him get it right...yes straining his self-knowledge-mirror-heat-knowledge-sand-into-glass-effect

AUDIENCE: HE'S! STILL! BREATHING!

[Setting:

The bus isn't coming. But it's too rainy to read. Walk to the next bus stop.

There's a bar under the bridge. It's called "Special Gravity" or "Specific Heat" or "Local Solar Time."

Sundials and shit on the walls.]

THE WILD KINDNESS

During the time I was in Seattle, researching Roethke, they thought my newest tumor was scar tissue. I had friends feel. It felt like muscle.

. . .

I wanted a scholastic diversion. I thought of Geoff Dyer's motive, in *Out of Sheer Rage*, his book about and not about D.H. Lawrence, to produce a "sober, academic study." He writes, "I can remember saying that word 'sober' to myself, over and over, until it acquired a hysterical, near-demented ring."

. . .

I wanted that scholastic rectitude to counter a certain wild feeling that has preceded each diagnosis. I could now diagnose a tumor by it, I think. It's probably a sign of general toxicity, comparable to the irregular heartbeat, disorientation, and fatigue of holistic renal strain. It produced a slight mania. We might think of dogs, ahead of a storm, trying to surge, senselessly, while they can. They might leap from the window to escape the thunder. Like yours did in that apartment in Holyoke that one winter. Pushed out the screen. The neighbor across the street would scream while snowblowing. He must have thought its sound would cover him.

. . .

It looked like running literally toward a blast, one afternoon. Like hearing a woman shout for someone to *stop stop* outside our apartment, some argument, and going outside with the long hammer. Waiting for those excuses, give me a reason. Like taping windows at the first hint of rain. Weeping at bees. I pulled over to help someone gather bales that had fallen from his truck, traffic whizzing, wanting the hay on my good shirt.

. . .

I don't often hear people talk about it, that wildness. Maybe that's because a lot of people don't survive, and others worry that reporting it could make them seem—or feel—erratic, unreliable, unrecoverable. I knew it from waiting rooms. My name was called, and the person next to me clutched my arm, made me promise we'd have dinner one day, one day, this place they knew.

. . .

I liked the emergency room doctor who said, "This isn't an emergency. You could've waited another hour." Then stabbed a thing into my lung.

. . .

I liked when M. showed up with a pineapple and a six-pack. "I always forget if you're allowed to drink in hospitals, like when someone gives birth, champagne," he said, opening a beer.

. . .

One night, looking for language that could stand when I couldn't stand language, the wildness led me to some lines by Roethke: "What book, O learned man, will set me right? / Once I read nothing through a fearful night." His poetry had helped me as an undergraduate, at that campus where he taught from 1947 to his death, Seattle. I thought it might help me again.

. . .

I love that "once" in "once I read nothing through a fearful night." It implies that every other fearful night, he read.

. . .

He was often manic in ways I've never known, running "from exhaustion to exhaustion." In and out of institutions. Thought he was a lion, went into a diner, ordered a raw steak.

. . .

"Try to imagine an elephant conducting Mozart superbly," a colleague said about him, a eulogy. I like to think of that conducting as electrical.

. . .

The wildness also made me sentimental. Or: in need of something, and it showed. I didn't know the drink the person in front me had at the Café Allegro. A new astringent concoction, espresso, seltzer, ice, tinctures, cream. I felt a surge of wild gratitude, to be alive in this year, after everything, to have survived to see this. I think she understood. "You have to try it, it's addicting," she said. And—unreasonable, thoughtless generosity of the pre-pandemic world, to be so received, regarded, for her to want me to find it addicting—this stranger offered a sip.

. . .

I started to say, "It means the world." I started to say, "Thanks for all time."

. . .

It also made me tired. Lunch with a friend. Told him I was crashing each day around 2 PM. He said, "Maybe tomorrow it will be 2:01." He didn't say the next day would be 2:02. The next day could be 1:50, the next could be darkness. That is, he wasn't suggesting optimism, improvement. He was suggesting endurance.

. . .

Dressing well in case I pass out on the train, thoughts like that. A bath takes a day to recover.

. . .

A feeling of sufficiency, sufficient displacement, hiding out, in my scholastic haunt. Washed my socks in the sink each night. Stored leftover rice in the half-finished yogurt tub: yogurt rice. Walked each morning to the archives.

. . .

My apartment was near the bar known as Roethke's bar. One of those places where, until recently, a friend said, you could pay with an advance on your paycheck but not use a credit card. Roethke was a legend there. A magisterial oil painting of him on one wall. "Roethke STD'd here" in the bathroom. A short recitation when someone saw what I was reading: "I knew a woman, lovely in her bones." He'd memorized it while working at the university, alone in a booth, making audio versions of textbooks. "It's hard to believe a poem could embrace so much," Jay Parini said.

. . .

One of the regulars (a ghost, or quoting a ghost) told me he didn't want to be rude but he'd never thought of Roethke as a regional poet of the Pacific Northwest. Rather, he was a regional poet of all the "non-regions" of the U.S. Anywhere that's rural but not necessarily agricultural, or not productively. Same songs on the radio, hits neither current nor classic. Same chain stores. He didn't want to be rude (I realized he meant it like "rudimentary"), but the main thing about the northwest, he said, is a non-thing, that "there's always a winter sky." But hardly any snow. Non-sky, a remove. "If I had to guess about Roethke," he said, "he was the kind of guy whose only interest in Mt. Rainier was that he might write a poem about it."

. . .

The mountain is framed, fantastically, above the fountain on campus. But you can't see it, most days—that "winter sky." And then it's there. I never would have written a poem about it in college. It would have seemed too obvious. But now I'm interested in the exactly-obvious. Assuming most early work fails for being under- or over-obvious. "Describe dogs," Roethke wrote in a notebook, "usual dogs."

. . .

The fog of illness. The fog doesn't dissipate but lifts. Is lifting. It is not uplifting, but it lifts you. You're in it. Thereabout.

. . .

Since I'd last been there, they'd installed ramps on the rim of the fountain. So ducks could get out.

HUGO SCENE, 9

> hey, Brad…did you hear about those monks who used to meditate for days on end staring at blank walls…and they'd see all sorts of trippy shapes and patterns and big insights and shit…and then these psychologists from SUNY Fredonia came to study visions and inspiration…and they had a bus full of the most far-out abstract painters of their day…to show these monks their far-out paintings…the idea was these monks had trained themselves to have their minds blown by blank walls…by nothing but air…so now this would be like getting the top-shelf unadulterated whiz-bang shit…and you know what the monks said…
>
> AUDIENCE: My kid could paint that!
>
> Hugo's book is an essential text of creative writing pedagogy…

SECOND LECTURE

Let's try something different tonight. Like we have a choice! Happiness, I think, can be called rapidity of thought. Well, up to a point. Or maybe happiness is itself what calls. And that call—its *calling*—can feel like rapidity of thought? Roethke picks up that call. "I proclaim once more a condition of joy," he says. The condition of "I proclaim once more a condition" can itself, in the best times, feel like joy. Let the conditions claim us. Let them clam us? Not "clam us up," but "clam" us, as in, "happy as a." Put the clams or clamps where you'll feel them most. Yum. OK, we're getting associative, yeah? Briny. That's good. Quick, let's see who can invent the most creative new flavor of Pringles?

AUDIENCE: Hot asphalt?

AUDIENCE: Sour pennies?

AUDIENCE: Margarita-last-sip-of-straw-sucking-sound?

That's good—the sound is a flavor. That's sound. And pretty funny. We'll be wailing in our seats. I mean that like "whaling," too. Clams, whaling—what a savings! And you know what wailing in the seat sounds like (*mouth-fart sound*).

(AUDIENCE *mouth-farts here and there.*)

OK, I think we're ready. So, David Wagoner, the

poet-teacher-novelist, student of Roethke's, editor of selections from Roethke's notebooks—Wagoner wrote this play about Roethke, *First Class*. In his intro, he talks about how Roethke, in his more manic or "grandiose phases," would call people on the telephone. The president of his university. The mayor of Seattle. The governor. Poets—to recite poems at them. Who would you like to call? So I brought these—

> (*Lifts sizable cardboard box labeled PHONES in black marker.*)

They're all just shoes. Let me pass them around. In this world, every shoe is also a phone. That's a reference to—well, it's just true. It's also a reference to a time Roethke was in some extremity and showed up, after this transportive but rupturing walk, and he was missing a shoe. Lots of options in here, what kind of phone do you want?

> (*Pulls out a big variety, like a rubber boot, starlet-red stiletto, one that's a "smart" or "dumb" shoe, a smelly tennis shoe, then...a fish? Smells it, likes the smell, tries to put it on his foot, etc.*)

"I don't have to teach you how to swallow a fish. Or do I? Headfirst or you'll strangle." That's from Wagoner's play.

> (*To be clear, what's happening is he has a box full of shoes. And the idea is each shoe is a phone. And each shoe-phone*

> *has a lecture about Roethke recorded inside it. People are going to hold up the shoe-lecture-phones to their ears and let the shoe-phones' tongues lick their ears as they listen to lectures and he's gonna come around and listen in and report what the lectures are saying.)*

Let's make this more like a classroom.

> *(Unfolds sizable cardboard box cut into a single flat piece, sets it up like a chalkboard, gets out his black marker, sloppily scrawls CHALKBOARD on it.)*

This is what we can do when there's neither fiddle nor squeezebox for the dancing, as Roethke said. They say creativity works like this. First, "immersion." You gotta be in it. And then "impasse." You get stuck. That's also necessary. Let's get stuck more. What's the sound of one shoe clopping? How many phones in a shoebox does it take to make it a phone-box? Do you prefer the idea of "getting stuck more" or "getting more stuck"? Muck a muck a muck a muck—I'm working on it. The muck a muck a muck a muck stuck a much could suck a muck your shoe. Could shuck the oyster muck of you, uh. Impasse. And then you need "diversion." That's step three, after "immersion," after "impasse." Look around.

> *(Very overtly performs peering at audience.)*

Or take a shower. Take a hike. Hike!

> (*Gestures like hiking football, throws self pass, crashes a bit through chairs to catch it, fumbles imaginary ball, despondent, pathetic, making the effort, like every moment he's in control frightens him because it increases the chances that he will soon not be in control, or will need to be balanced out by who knows what?*)

And then stage four: "insight!" So, if you're interested in insight, you need to get stuck, get diverted. That's what I want to try tonight. There's just too much I want to get into—that's what's gotten into me. First, we'll make it even more like a classroom.

> (*Unfolds other sizable pieces of cut-up cardboard. The logic is that using cardboard and markers is what "makes things into a classroom." For example, he drapes one cut-up box over the lectern, scrawls LECTERN on it. The lectern is now a lectern in a classroom.*)

I had this dream. We were all at a university and they were unloading syllabi from the back of a truck. The deans were. This is a reference to something I saw once—all these street performers and vendors just kinda randomly getting their day's props and assignments. Here, you take a bucket of roses to sell. You take a saxophone. And they were making teaching assignments this way. I got a syllabus called "The History of Theatrical Dance." I started lecturing. Well, first I started with free-writing. Well, first I had them make a shape that they thought would be more conducive to our topic—to move the desks into a shape. Then we did free-writing for like forty-five minutes. Just keep your pens moving! And I got the classroom ready.

> (*Uses cardboard to get the classroom-within-a-classroom ready, layering cardboard to make a projector, a screen, a cardboard marker labeled MARKER, etc.*)

I'm, like, fiddling with the projector, a great way to buy time, and I do the bit where I, like, make little jokes. Like about using technology. And then in an off-hand but totally rehearsed way, I'm like, "I'd love to see a play made of nothing but what professors say while they're fiddling with a projector."

(*Laughter*)

And someone's like, "If I write that play and get an A can I never come back to this class?" And I'm like, "Only if you take me with you!"

(*Laughter*)

And then I start teaching. I was teaching that whole time,

but then I start really getting into it: "Welcome! It's so good to see you all. This is one of my favorite courses to teach, The History of Theatrical Dance. What is the history of theatrical dance? Thoughts? We'll get into this more next week, but just as a preview, one theory about the History of Theatrical Dance is how key it is to history, to theatre, and also to dance."

> (*Draws three-circle Venn diagram on cardboard projector screen, also drawing some lines to represent beams of light from the projector, making beam-of-light sounds.*)

"And that doesn't even get into whether a particular item or artifact or feeling or what in this class we'll call, in every case, a *text* is closer to history-theatre or theatre-dance or dance-theatre or whatever. Also, let's not forget you could have history-dance-theatre or theatre-theatre-theatre-history-dance, and lots more. And then you could ask what would it take—within or around a text—to shift it or to shift our perception of it to, like, dance-dance-history-theatre-dance. That's a big theory in the field. How to turn that dial. We'll get into that a lot. But I think it's always useful to start out with what things aren't. And with our past experiences. And with what our past experiences aren't." Then I have them make a list of things that aren't history or theatre or dance, and things that are and also things that aren't their past experiences. Then they free-write about their lists. Then they compare their lists and their free-writing about their lists with a partner. Then they free-write about their experiences with comparing with a partner, and they share that free-writing in small groups, then they small-group-write. Then we focus on time management for a while, like, for a really long time, and do some reflective writing about time management. I love teaching. We don't have time to really get into it tonight, but it's interesting to go back to Roethke's writing about teaching. There's been a lot of good critique of conventions of creative writing pedagogy lately. But what he says about teaching—it mostly just sounds reasonable, at least when he's not trying to be funny. It'd work today. Progressive. "The class in writing poetry is a collective, collaborative act."

But today we'll use these phones to choose-our-own-adventure through some different lectures. Does everyone have one? Or you could use your own, if your shoe has a lecture in it.

> (*This is when he starts going around, leaning close to audience members, cheek to cheek, listening to the shoe-lecture-phones up to their ears. And things can happen like maybe someone isn't playing along, and the shoe-lecture-phone is in their lap, so he puts his ear on their lap. Or he gets confused and tries to listen to shoe-shoes on people's*

> *actual feet. Or he shakes one shoe-lecture-phone and a smaller shoe-lecture-phone falls out with a tiny lecturing voice inside, etc.)*

OK (*leaning into a shoe/audience member*), so this first lecture returns us to last night. About Jack Spicer. Spicer, specter, scepter. "Spicer can be broader in his groaners and slicker in his winking," it's saying. "The idiom differs, but there's a similar mix of the obvious and of quick pivots in many of Roethke's most livewire, fuse-strewn moments." "Fuse-strewn" is nice. Burke says Roethke has fusions and confusions and diffusions. The diffusions sometimes outweigh, he says. He doesn't say that's a bad thing. He says, "The method may be further extended by the use of a word in accordance with pure pun-logic." Quick, let's try to apply "pure pun-logic" to the phrase "pure pun-logic."

> (*Sounds out possibilities slowly, with different accents, touching his face to help it make shapes to help pronunciation, etc.*)

Puurrre punnn-logggic. Piiiieeer pin Legos. Pooooouur piiiine Legolas. Pioneeeeer pineal jig. I'll keep working on it. Academics, like dog owners, like to talk about training. My training is this. I have a lot of thoughts about how sounds become other sounds, or sons.

OK, this next lecture—it's a little snarky! It's saying that

Spicer and Roethke are closest when they give a sense of "playing ping-pong without a net—or with a paddle wrapped in it." Or maybe they mean "rapt" in it, "r-a-p-t," like a hawk? "The ball smacked every which way. So different tables and boundaries emerge, depending on how it bounces. Bop. Closer to a neural network than to Frost's famous court, no barrier holding forth, or back, or back and forth, between pulse and prefrontal glitter." Now they're quoting Roethke: "'I'm king of the boops!' What's Spicer king of? Among other things, The Forest: 'Look I am King Of The Forest / Says The King Of The Forest…My right leg / Does not fit my left leg.' 'Don't tell my hands,' Roethke says in a moment of comparable discombobulation. Beckett might come to mind. But only as much as he always should. Body finding itself, what it is, as it comes to pieces. Echolocating by 'boop' and 'look.'"

"Pure-pun logic"…would "ping-pong allergic" work? It's close. I used to know the difference between a pun and a rhyme, and why most things people call puns aren't really. I used to know that so well, I didn't need to remember it anymore.

I didn't think it'd be so crowded in here. (*Noticing all the cardboard…*) There's room on the piano bench. And probably inside it. If you're feeling *like* music. You know, when they came for all his stuff, to truck it to the archives, they left the piano. The music was too heavy. OK, another lecture (*leans close to someone*). Oh, wait, did you make a personal call? And that's what they're saying to you? You like to be talked to that way?

(*Laughter*)

Moving on…this one's about Lorine Niedecker. Really strange that her work doesn't come up more, in connection with Roethke. Poets of the Upper Midwest. Great Lakes. Born a few years before him, died a few years after. Wisconsin to his Michigan. But she stayed. Anyone here from Wisconsin? Poets of landscape, a Midwest past its initial boom. But booming into our current sense of it. Their poetry is especially cousinly in its relationship to nursery rhyme and to self-soothing, self-singing rhythms from childhood, metabolized beyond Modernism. They can be read as proto-postmodernists. But with an eye, also, to the jump ropes thwapping down the street. That is, with a feeling that the poet might run out and jump into those ropes. It won't go well. It might just be a circus. However quiet. But what revelatory tangles. OK, now there's a close reading of some passages of near-rhyme from both poets, of how their poems shift in and out of ballad. The rhyme sounds from Niedecker are "sud- / love / tub." From Roethke, "moo / who / coo." "Rhyming is the avoidance of mental pain by addicting yourself to what will happen next," as Nicholson Baker says. Now the lecture is talking about these lines from Niedecker—"Something in the water / like a flower / will devour / water / flower." Which performs, they say, "leaps and lulls of composition." A kind of thinking, on the page. The residues of song glitch into emphasis, they're saying. And dissolve. Connects it to Roethke's lines, "I run to the whistle of money. // Money money money / Water water water." Notational ripples. Fuse and diffuse.

OK, one more?

> (*Finds a really huge comedically extravagant shoe that someone is holding up to their ear. Maybe it's also cardboard,* labeled SHOE, *with SHOE crossed out,* labeled PHONE?)

Rhapsody means "to weave," they're saying. This one is about Christopher Smart, John Clare. Mad-song. The music of electric subjectivity, Blake's idea of not seeing with the eye but through it. They're quoting Roethke, in his epigrammatic third-person mode: "The only wisdom he acquired from poetry [was] a special wisdom of feeling, not a refinement of feeling." That's important: wisdom without refinement. *A* wisdom. That's probably one of our central themes. That is, there may be a conclusion, a thing learned and stated, wisdom, but without conclusive fiddling. The fiddling has been for transmission, not refinement. The feelings are not refined, because they're full at each turn. Nothing will be on the test; everything has been a test. They're connecting this to more "elliptical" recent poetry. To "wit" that may look like wisdom, in time, and keep us busy in the meantime.

It passes the time. It passes for time. And they're talking about recent work of fractured or sustained song—or the fractures are sustained. You can run on them. They bear. Adrienne Raphel. Douglas Kearney. Olena Kalytiak Davis. Her poems, they're saying, at times answer Roethke's regression in a maternal mode ("must our hips be hips / for children to sit on?"), among a lot else they do.

Oh, I wanted to find the lecture about Roethke counting himself among the "happy poets." It compares him to E.E. Cummings. Or as I pronounce it, "Eeeeeeeeee." I think it's in a loafer? An inviting loafer, "I loaf and invite...my sole." There's another fish for you. Roethke was a poet of struggle, that lecture says, who often, in a poem, found his way to moments of ease, whereas Cummings was a poet of ease, or who wanted it, who dressed it up in struggle? Struggle syntactic or typographic. Something like that. In Roethke, the dress-up is more serious, more private? Like a child garbed in seriously giddy or agitated chatter, spinning alone in the yard, costumed in spinning, spinning and catching, caught and spinning and catching. Potato bugs and sun tea. His biographer says he respected Cummings because he "blew up the language." Roethke doesn't "blow up" language. Well, maybe like you'd try to blow up a hot air balloon. When you're in the air, soaring, and it starts to deflate! Blow into it! Come on, you lungs! Like blowing into a nascent fire, or ear. A shell.

This lecture's just wind, windy windful wind. OK, one more.

There's a good one somewhere about tone, what Frost called "sentence sounds." You can hear a phrase through a half-open door. Or in a half-tied shoe. And you get the drift. The gesture. The content is gesture. "I can't catch a bush," Roethke says. You might half-hear the sound of "I can't catch a break." Or, maybe, "I can't catch a bus." And that locates us, in tone. But the phrase also obliterates the anchoring sound. That is, it uses a known phrasal and tonal gesture-pattern but also swivels totally, or tonally, because of the words inside that shape. Because what could it "mean" to "catch a bush"? So the shape gives solidity, plausibility, reality, a tone that we know, while the diction torques. An effect of counterpoint. Or like when he says, of his father: "He watered the roses. His thumb had a rainbow." That's intuitive and smart without or despite knowing it. There's the idiom of having a "green thumb." You don't hear that, not exactly, in "his thumb had a rainbow." But it's an underlying pulse, harmonic specter cascading about. About is what it's about. It's a rainbow. That lecture draws a lot on Natalie Gerber's writing on tone, very good scholarship, and Kate Greenstreet's poetry. She's so good.

There were other shoes here, too. Like one about his "minimals"—he becomes small, and he becomes *snail*. How scale is "acquired" in his work, as in "the sun for me glinted the sides of a sand grain." It's like he's suddenly smaller than a grain of sand. That's overwhelming, but it can also feel good to be overwhelmed—would somebody like to come up and hold my wrist against the mantle for a minute? It's nice to be tied up in thought.

What else? "Can a cat milk a hen?" Roethke asks. I love that. It's so pragmatic! I forget what lecture it's in. I guess it's in this one now, my own. Maybe it's the lecture that's playing in a pair of slippers? Who has the slippers-phone? Slippers, which, in Roethke, a critic said, should be heard as "slip-ooze." Silky. Or silkie—the kind of chicken, if we're clucking in that direction. Anyway, "can a cat milk a hen?" It's like he knows what things are, and he knows about their potential relationships, but he doesn't know how those match up. It's like he needs to milk this hen, but he only has a cat to do it. How? And who's he asking? What authority? It's sincere, and pretty funny. That kind of uncleverment, at the limits of intelligence. It brings us to the kind of impasse I mentioned earlier, following immersion, setting us up for insight. It calls back to Blake, to Shakespearean fools.

AUDIENCE: Brad, would you add Yeats's Crazy Janes to what you've been saying?

Maybe? Maybe not. Since a deliberately this-is-persona persona is different? Roethke's "Meditations of an Old Woman" might come to mind. As Don Bogen said, "Listening for the voice of an ostensibly fictional character" helped "his development of a new 'meditational' mode." For Yeats the persona lets him wild out. For Roethke, it calms. He was already singing. He didn't need a guise for that.

AUDIENCE: Was he Confessional? I sometimes hear he was. But if so, what's he confessing to?

Well, "I'm a biscuit." He confesses to that.

(*Laughter*)

AUDIENCE: Yes, but the point of a confession is usually to reveal something, then get some purification, or absolution, penance, or at least you've purged it. But he's just talking to flowers.

Well, a real confession should get you arrested. The problem with most Confessional poets is they weren't arrested more? But maybe he's just confessing *to*. Endstop. Like, he's confessing to the flowers, to his hands, to the goldy grass, to rhyme? The point is toward. The content is gesture, a body to find—the tone of each phrase helps us find the body? He roves awesomely around that tonal dial—that's back to "sentence sounds" again. We already heard that lecture.

AUDIENCE: I'm interested in the Niedecker connections. It doesn't seem like direct influence, but more ambient. That's a lot of what you're talking about: influence isn't, like, the seeds, planted, seeds we brought deliberately from here to there. But the ones that blow over the fence.

Yes, and sometimes an entire sapling might blow over. A whole orchard. Or it could hitch a ride in a rabbit's gut. What? This bunny shit a whole orchard. Or the flower in one place might remind you of another.

AUDIENCE: Of another flower? Or another place?

Just—of another. I is another. You never know when someone else might be around. As Roethke says, "*You may be Dirty Dinky!*" We could do worse than all draw who or what we think Dirty Dinky is for a thousand years. It reminds me of my favorite AI captioning fail from one of his poems. Roethke says, "And we dance on, dance on, dance on." And the captions say, "And we dance on, Anton, Anton."

(*Laughter*)

So, Anton might be in the poem, whether you know it or not. Watch out for Anton.

AUDIENCE: These connections start to feel a little breezy, coincidental. Are you just talking about a general mood?

Moods ring, I think. Should we answer? And one way out of scholarly ruts is to dig them wider, let some wind in? Find a buried stream, let it flood you out? Make sure you float, or can breathe underwater. Or you could flatten that pit to a foundation, build there. But I do think the mood is the main thing. Or the mood is the *mean* thing. As in, what it all reverts to. It cuts through. Here he is in "Give Way, Ye Gates":

> *Believe me, knot of gristle, I bleed like a tree;*
> *I dream of nothing but boards;*
> *I could love a duck.*

Quack quack. It's not surprising to hear a related zagging quickness—it's the folk tradition, fast as song—in, say, Bob Dylan. I'm getting a little tired-hungry-bored. A little why'd-I-ever-do-this-research-and-where-could-it-lead. I mean, besides being here. Which I wanted to do? Or I wanted what I imagined could happen *after* I was here? Where's that? Though I was hoping we'd talk about the criticism that Roethke isn't "political." That is, in terms of certain kinds of social realism, position papers, even though he writes about the "inexorable sadness of pencils" and office work, pickle factory work, all that. And chums, neighbors. Animals, ecology. That'd be an interesting lecture—maybe I'll do that one instead of this one, if there's a second time? He was accused of preferring "the mad microcosm of a private sensibility." But folks like Rosemary Sullivan, pretty early, noted that he "felt more than is generally supposed the pressure toward a poetry of social concern." And Quetchenbach nicely makes the case that you can read his poetry in terms of "the ineffectiveness of its attempts to engage politics." That's interesting—how the poetry fails at being political, that's part of the political. Social-rhetorical-artistic forms might not work. And seeing that is itself political. We fell apart, what we had didn't work, or things wouldn't let it, it couldn't work, but we tried, or tried to try, and it all happened in places. And in us. And we survived it, in our ways, as much as we could. And at times, let's say, poems did work, or did the work of trying to work. We believed it. If you can believe that. That all sets us up to think about Roethke as an ecopoet. Since how can we "succeed" in addressing the most extreme states of, like, climate, its objects too large to think? And the particulars of a "mad microcosm" and a "private sensibility" reveal and reflect and result from social conditions, and so on. In his archive, there's a book on tort law, probably from his brief stint in law school. He finished the program, as we say, meaning he dropped out. He underlined, "No duty was imposed on them until the trespasser was discovered in a position of peril." The route to duty, to responsibility, begins in peril? So, if you wish to be responsible, you should seek ruin? That reminds me of George Herbert's reflections on the pastoral obligation to understand sin, firsthand, if possible. So Roethke found himself in hard positions, which obliterated how and why he could be responsible, could even *be*—so then he played a caricature of himself, at times, to try to regain a responsible role, while refraining from its worst terms? The refrain brings us back. Or, he stayed responsible—to poems? To a faith in that? A need? What's the difference between faith and need?

Or I could just list occasions of ducks in Roethke for a bit? Where's the duck phone? Aaron M. Moe writes about Roethke's turn to the "zoopoetical." Discusses an aphorism by Roethke that never tells us "what, exactly, is like the minnow," so that what is "like the minnow" becomes, he suggests, the aphorism itself. That brings Rae Armantrout to mind, for some reason. Is this all lecturing is? Being together, in words? Or words being together, in us? "A duck knows something / You and I don't. / Tomorrow is Friday." Is Roethke saying the duck knows it's Friday? No, but the duck knows something. We don't. And "love's light as a duck," and "I could love a duck." I could love that "could." He's offering himself to the possibility. He'll put his back into it, he could be the cat that milks the hen, he's up for it, give him a call. Any last thoughts? Then tomorrow I'll get into my actual scholarship. I hope this was the diversion, or is it the impasse? Maybe it's immersion-impasse-diversion altogether? Yes?

CARYL: Yes well...I was thinking...can I say something about Niedecker?

> (CARYL *moves radiantly/haltingly through the chairs to the lectern, passing out papers. Stands beside the lectern. She's carrying a cardboard box labeled BACKPACK in black marker. It contains a large stack of papers, rocks, small tree sticking out like a single palm tree in a cartoon drawing of a desert island. This is the actual Caryl Pagel, a*

separate actual person, actually about to speak.)

CARYL'S LECTURE

CARYL: I was thinking about your description of Roethke's ping-pong singsong, his internal locomotion as galoot-whistling-a-continuous-tune, tempestuous wind, and how these sound games for Niedecker also rely on forms of listening. Gossip, birdsong, friendship, haiku. Tap tap tap on the window, errant exchange, side of the road.

Niedecker's rhymes—in addition to those you just mentioned with their purposeful ice block endings melting—often also bind bits of overheard chitchat in what for her's been dubbed a "folk tradition." Language as material that falls out of people. Speech acts. Proximity. Place as form. She was always lifting sillies from friends, family, neighbors—the fatty organic conversation then condensed in the process of writing, richer through thickening, like sweetened milk in a dairy plant (her joke). I've always liked the word "folk" and its connection to the ordinary talk of the public's potential: civil rights histories, tall or twice-told tales, her neck of the woods' Sewer Socialism, labor songs—though worry it sometimes signals too swiftly "poor" or "rural." Here's a poem from *New Goose*, LN's first book, which was published in 1946 though mostly written in the Depression-era '30s:

> *Mr. Van Ess bought 14 washcloths?*
> *Fourteen washrags, Ed Van Ess?*

*Must be going to give em
to the church, I guess.*

*He drinks, you know. The day we moved
he came into the kitchen stewed,
mixed things up for my sister Grace—
put the spices in the wrong place.*

Here the rhyme's arising straight from snark and regional pun-slang ("stewed!"), making fun of lumbering local wealth's bad taste as it manifests in poor manners. Your sins toward women are shooting down the grapevine, Ed Van Ess—your name itself new insult. Get it, Brad? And those great, familiar grips of intimacy: sass gets an "I guess" while gossip's launched with "you know." We're right there. Wouldn't miss it. The ladies guild's revenge from inside the bean making.

Niedecker loved music.

Do you like music, Brad?

> (*Doesn't wait for* BRAD *to respond...*)

Niedecker's lifelong best friend, a poet—we'll call him "Zuk," as she did—was married to a composer with whom he had a child prodigy violinist kid whose career Niedecker devotedly followed. She even wrote a book for him! *For Paul and Other Poems*, it was called. Her second collection, in her lifetime unpublished. Unlike Roethke, there was no piano in her home but she acquired a record player and listened to Duke Ellington, Vivaldi,

Beethoven (whom she was embarrassed for loving, too pedestrian), writing: "Chopin's Etudes (o exquisite—there need not be anything else in the world for me—just let me have a phonograph before I turn over my body and soul to the country!)." Referring to Mozart, LN also writes she's drawn to "all that music that I never seem to grasp but always transports" and "I love it because I feel that I think this way, not *thought* but everything in a movement of words."

On the one hand, Niedecker's poems explore the Objectivist/post-Imagist notion that a cool intellectual look at material conditions is what poetry is after. On the other, there's Niedecker's idea that "for myself, what is deeper than I understand is often the most pertinent to me and the most lasting," and so the material—the suds, the eaves, the owl, the rags—leads one into and through the absorbing and enigmatic songs of experience.

It's like what you said, Brad, or what I heard in one of the shoes, about the spin and dip of Roethke's poems "all becoming circular, but intimate experiences, mystical experiences," and how those poems "connect to the social—they circle us." We are the processed mulch of our collective moments! Who said that? Later in life Niedecker wrote she was "much taken up with how to define a way of writing poetry which is not Imagist nor Objectivist fundamentally nor Surrealism alone," but where "the basis is direct and clear—what has been seen or heard," and then also, she continues, "something gets in, overlays all that to make a state of consciousness . . . A light, a motion, inherent in the whole." Not thought. *Movement*. Perhaps her poetics is best expressed in this little four-line ditty, one of my favorites, let's all read it together:

> (*It takes a while to pass the papers around, but eventually everyone has one and reads more or less together*):

Remember my little granite pail?
The handle of it was blue.
Think what's got away in my life—
Was enough to carry me thru.

The object, the item, the idea—it's all ephemeral, transient, losable, gone. Everything changes, every *thing* is capable of ruin or escape ("throw *things* / to the flood" she famously writes later). What's important, this poem wants us to know, is that as we stumble from one tool or scene or toy to the next (experience), the language or hum of our losses (objects, memories, ideas) *carry* us—the release itself transportive, impelling one's ear to the next thought. I mean spot! I mean music, its movement. It worms you through you. Rhyme's bet (if "every word rhymes," which LN would agree with) is that letting go is itself survival.

BRAD: To be more clear, I think the core of things is—every word rhymes, but it's also important to believe it matters that one word isn't another. To believe it matters whether we say one word "isn't another" or "isn't any other." Every word rhymes, and radiates, jostles, wrings. But you also need to keep finding your way back to understand that every word rhymes *because* it matters that this word you are saying isn't another—

CARYL: Yes, right. And it's nice to imagine Teddy and Lorine—just two American kids, growin' up in the heartland—writing rambunctious rhythmic colloquial pieces, him teasing a chorus of Dinky demons, her catching rumble from rumor, as contrast to the less social (in one sense) ego-focused psychological noodling of their contemporaneous East Coast Confessional poet peers (if we're going to be Team Regional about it!). But, I also think there's a different kind of pressure to being a joker in a skirt. Or a differently perceived pressure to writing witty social-critical poems as a rural working single Midwestern woman, poems that for Niedecker are mostly read and received during her lifetime by a small and *serious* academic male audience…

Wait.

Did everyone get my handout?

(CARYL *squints into the distance.*)

AUDIENCE: The poem?

CARYL: No, the other one.

Oh, well, nevermind. The point I'm heading toward is

something about how she was writing into and from a social situation, a folk tradition, but it wasn't the social situation of her readers. Roethke, an obvious outsider in his vibrant aesthetic range and odd behaviors, was still writing from "inside" the mainstream publishing/prize-winning/academic Poetry Community of their time. Niedecker was—intentionally and circumstantially—both always in touch with and still very far removed from any IRL literary engagements. She caught glimpses. It's complicated. I won't go on…I bring up her positioning not so much for biographical reasons but aesthetic. I've wondered if writing a poem with nursery rhyme architecture or a silly sonic joke can deflate expectations—which is one way of surpassing them. Humor and music as decoy. Wry formal torque. Hot dog in the maw. Like: don'tchya worry, Brad, this lil gal Lorine just writes children's rhymes. Nothing to see here!, Brad!,—as LN tucks sharp shards of resistance into her lullabies, many of *New Goose*'s poems boiling down (the milk! the beans!) to Fuck the Police or Damn the Man, familiar domestic forms harboring political stances (often through the voices of others) about land rights, housing, war, poverty, hunger, or rural economics. It's there if you want it.

If not, there's other levity available. Here's a quick one, also from *New Goose*—(I guess I could talk about her later longer poems another day, if Brad ever invites me back!)—a poem slick in sound, easy to digest, and also cynically, "anonymously" exploring the hypocrisy and impracticality of war-time government's insults to its citizens, the forthcoming "stop it" both softened by the hard/obvious rhyme of "profit" and made harsher, angrier, stronger by it:

> *I doubt I'll get silk stockings out*
> *of my asparagus*
> *that grows too fast to stop it,*
> *or any pair of Capital's*
> *miracles of profit.*

New Goose's folk works are often locally sourced in her home of Blackhawk Island but LN was also working with the WPA in Madison around this time, the oral histories of those culture-mapping projects a clear influence. We might call what she's up to "documentary" now. Another aspect of "folk art" that LN plays with in earlier poems is assuming the position of Anonymous, absenting the particularities of the self in service of direct message, a presentation of the public or open sourced. In this poem "I" is anyone, everyone whose been gaslit or confused by distant or irrelevant governmental policies, and "Capital" is the singular villain. The Dirty Dinky in DC.

That reminds me: back to what I was saying about Roethke and LN—she had many poet friends but a limited poetry community. She published with small presses in a slow and chaotic manner, and while her all-male poet buds privately embraced her writing they did little to support her work in meaningful material ways. Her Objectivist pals were often too busy to mention her to publishers or write an introduction or harness their own power in literary circles to speed something up. Her friends admired her, but from my point of view her poetics, innovations, and career were often an afterthought.

Niedecker's archives are currently scattered among various libraries, her remaining photos, notes, and papers kept within male peers' or publishers' archives. This fact disappoints—that she isn't honored with a single archival home, that each curious Niedecker-loving weirdo has to patch together the scraps anew—but one can't say it doesn't suit her, or that she didn't make choices toward privacy (asking Al, her late-in-life husband, to burn her journals after she died; trashing the letters between her and Zuk during their romantic youth; not giving public talks or readings), or that she wouldn't get the joke. No one could say she didn't help set it up. In fact, in 1969, just before she died, she sold a pile of correspondence between her and Zuk to the Harry Ransom Center at UT Austin, building a garage on her and Al's Blackhawk property with the proceeds. Henceforth they called their carpark "University of Texas."

Whelp! On that note.

> (CARYL *claps hands or slaps knees in a gesture of moving-along-ness.*)

Is it time for the Roadhouse pub crawl yet? To wrap this

up, Niedecker's aim was to remain, as a poet, more-or-less unseen, reserved. She had confidence in and ambition for the work, wanting her books to be published and read—but no wish to perform them. Perhaps because the language wasn't only hers. She's sure of her writing's import but doesn't care to act the character. No teaching or prize-winning readings. It might be ironic: a folk author with no public relationship to an audience—but if folk is meant in part to reflect, perhaps one's meant to keep their own personality…if not *out of it*, more like the pail that carries, this point of view an intentionally useful and inclusive erasure—a perspective more familiar to her gender?

I mean…What do I know?!

> CARYL *sits on the floor and waits a long time.*

[Setting:

Overheard conversation at the next table. They're sure they know each other from somewhere. They go through the circumstances: high school, the gym, that one blood bank. Do you also lose everything at the casino? No, no, no.

Eventually, one asks if they ever come to this very bar. Yes, all the time! Me too! We met here last week.]

HUGO SCENE, 10

we're past mortality now…in the archive…it already happened…in the university…it's too dark to read…so we fall back on our training…dark jokes…falling onto our educations like…any old sword…hey, Brad…did you hear about the pioneer who was mad because…

(BRAD *voice*) why was he mad…

he was mad because this woman showed up and he was like…"I thought I ordered a mail-order *bridge*"…

we actually prefer speaking this way…to sing below the tension of the lyre…to ask three questions at once so in response you can say whatever you want…to speak below the bellows of a pun…I guess my philosophy is…self-knowledge isn't something you have…it's something others have about you…I think of when I played Prospero in my first major theatrical ambition…lots of connections to that…

(BRAD *voice*) "a creature who could write but couldn't read"…

as Hugo said…

(BRAD *voice*) can I have a kiss…

unfortunately, Brad, we're out of hot dogs

    (*smooths* BRAD)

but what Hugo loved most was tone...and maybe *The Triggering Town* is basically about a triggering tone, a harmonic glitch, which tunes and extends... he wrote it in the posture of a professor...which he became at pains after he turned forty...he felt like he was faking it at the beginning...imitating Roethke in the classroom...

but I think in this moment things have shifted... people still talk about imposter syndrome...which maybe is what Hugo felt...starting as a professor after a career at Boeing...but now we're more in the era of "I'm competent and over-qualified but the system around me has severely limited the possibilities or forces me to act in particular ways to leverage strategic utility in a matrix of precarity austerity everyone is disposable" syndrome...

so he has big Roethke-was-my-teacher energy...and also that Wakefield energy...looking out the window at a house across the street where your wife thinks you're dead...put those two energies together...

the feeling that this is the most we can do...given everything...this rowing with feathers...flying with oars...

    (BRAD *voice*) hey, what do you call the speedy

online fish and chips store that only takes orders by email…e-ficcient chips…what do you call the Indian restaurant in Saginaw where they deliver your sag paneer on the side of a bicycle… Saginaw Pannier… hey, who was Andy Warhol's favorite cowboy clown…Kansas Oops…

but it can still happen…the transformative…like one day I got lost in this meadow I'm permitted to return to most days…the literary thought is what must have failed…where else must I have tried to go… to go there every day and…to have time to go there every day or…I didn't have time to…but I went…

HUGO SCENE, 11

our last mini-game is a dating sim mash-up puzzle game...Brad will be playing a person playing a taffy-slapping puzzle game on his phone while on dates... and if he stops playing...well then the firefighters will come and take his date off to college...

but his dates don't know that...his dates want him to pay attention to them...they'll leave if he doesn't... they got a babysitter, took the night off, are very attracted to him...so he has to keep them there... meaning pay attention to them...but he also has to ignore them and play the taffy-slapping game on his phone...or else the firefighters will come and take his dates to college...but he also has to make conversation...if they leave we know what will happen to them...they want to leave folks they really do...but not like that...

Brad doesn't want that either do you Brad...though an implied dynamic is...how long will he have the heart...

he could try to explain the situation but good luck...reference to Keanu in *Speed*, 1994...which it turns out was exactly twenty-three years after Chris Burden with those electric ladders, huh...

meanwhile back to Hugo...the point isn't a portrait...

it's the view from the subject…what do we see…silos…a bad motel…how the vines in the take-out joint were painted by hand…the owner's daughter loves to paint…Brad is thinking he could stay and teach her perspective…

the cohesive element, as Hugo called it, is that we go on…you were saying something…you were saying something so the next thing applies…this faith in consistency, a consistency that emerges…it makes him closer to Hejinian and Stein than people think, closer to experimental shit…

he had to cite people in *The Triggering Town* and he sometimes cited poems worse than what he meant…we write the names we go by…we have our pride…we ventriloquize…

> (MABLE) it's really good we got to go on this date…it will be fun to be on a date…it's good to do something fun, don't you think…do you want to know my one weakness.

> (BRAD *voice*) I'm so nervous…I really hope she likes me…I spent fifteen minutes today trying on different lanyards…well, that's up to you…

> (MABLE) sweets…I can definitely be bribed with candy…I'm trusting you with this dangerous knowledge that can be used to manipulate me…would you like to decorate my room…

(BRAD *voice, to* AUDIENCE) my kid could paint that!...

HUGO SCENE, 12

the word Hugo actually uses is "adhesive"…"when you are writing you must assume that the next thing you put down belongs not for reasons of logic, good sense, or narrative development, but because you put it there. You, the same person who said that thing, also said this. The adhesive force is your way of writing"…

describe the distances between "cohesive" and "adhesive"…what kind of light is there in each… keep in mind that directly imitative concrete poetry often neutralizes the visual effect…you see the poem in the shape of a flower so you stop "seeing" in the ways that happen when language has no shape but language…put that in your this-is-not-a-pipe and smoke it…here come the firefighters…

AUDIENCE: HE'S! STILL! BREATHING!

tomorrow we'll focus on the detective novel Hugo wrote, *Death and the Good Life*…further evidence of his interest in tone over plot…or tone as plot… what crops up in the nonlinear voice…we'll try a dramatization…make sure to do your stretches, Brad…and then we'll have one more night…the need to survive, unfortunately, is perpetual…

but don't worry folks things aren't defined by how

things end…I've been wrong so often it's safest to assume the opposite…we might substitute, along the way, a lack of fulfillment with a fulfilling lack…reverence, to my thinking, is intransitive…though most things to my thinking are intransitive…they don't get through…but with reverence, I think, we don't have reverence *for*…we have reverence…period…postmodern or messianic…the critical gap is sunny…awe in spite of awe…

zenithal light, they call it, the light that happens from above…I don't know why we need a term for it…the light from above…this morning, for instance, weren't we very happy…weren't we all very happy folks…walking in rain, no reason…except a sense of middles…of being in middles…worms emerging along curbs…glowing like shards…they're also fans of middles…

[Setting:

The blur of taillights in rain. Phone in a plastic bag they gave you at the bar. The bartender offered a ride. It seemed nice to walk.

Rain picks up again. Stop in a doorway.

The feeling that if the door behind you opened, you would go in.]

WHAT BOOK

I made some minor discoveries in the archives in Seattle. For example, in *The Book of Common Prayer*, Roethke marked this line in pink: "Jesus said unto his disciples, Now I go my way." A source for his well-known line, "I learn by going where I have to go"?

. . .

As I researched him, his things, I found him researching himself. In a copy of *Antony and Cleopatra*, he marked the line, "You must think this, look you, that the worm will do his kind." He circled the second "you," wrote "Roethke" over it. In an anthology, he wrote "Roethke" beside Wordsworth's "Ode to Duty." And signed his name across the title page of *Reading Poems: An Introduction to Critical Study*—not as one would to indicate ownership, but as though to imply authorship, or something further. "I'm always sad not to be in an anthology," he wrote in a notebook.

. . .

And a fragment, in a margin: "The heart enchanted by my name." He didn't say "my heart." That's how you know he really meant "my heart."

. . .

Wordsworth's "Ode to Duty" begins with a quotation from Seneca: "I am no longer good through deliberate intent, but by long habit have reached a point where I am not only able to do right, but am unable to do anything but what was right." Roethke: "I feel my fate in what I cannot fear."

. . .

"Narcissism charming," he wrote next to a couplet by Kenneth Koch: "There is no midnight mystery / And no coconuts here to see." He then tried some lines in the style.

. . .

It happens most floridly in a copy of Stanley Kunitz's *Intellectual Things*, in which Roethke's annotations are closer to tagging, defacing, suggesting a cascading, whirling mood. He writes his name again and again. He crossed out "Kunitz" on one page, wrote "Roethke" over it on another. He's calling himself forth? Trying to hold himself together?

. . .

Jane Hirshfield describes a ninth-century monk, Zuigan, talking to himself each morning: "'Master Zuigan!' he would call out. 'Yes?' 'Are you here?' 'Yes!'" And Roethke wrote "Roethke."

. . .

Or it's like writing the name of a high school crush over and over in a notebook. But he wrote his own name. Kunitz, his mentor and friend, remarked that Roethke was not really a close observer, which Roethke's biographer says was fine, because "everything around him was useful to him only as signatures of himself." A poet of nature who, in any environment, got out of the car, sat down, stayed in one place.

. . .

Daffy notes, sometimes. What was he actually responding to? In an anthology of Beat poetry, he wrote: "Like the pike, like the hyena, these people are unkind." That may have been true, actually, but it appears next to a poem by Kerouac that ends with immense kindness: "everything is alright / forever and forever and forever, O thank you / thank you thank you."

. . .

I jotted my research in the margins of Roethke's collected poems, using it as a notebook, without regard for the text on the page. Like how Roethke wrote in books. I combined notes from the archives with lists, observations, personal reminders. I knew it looked strange; I hid it from librarians. Among the table of contents, for example, I wrote, "Arnold Stein: 'What contemplation was to some philosophers, composition was to Roethke.'" And: "S says the restaurant where he works is 2–3 years ahead of recent trends in pickling."

. . .

Roethke worked in a pickle factory. "The fruit rolled by all day. / They prayed the cogs would creep."

...

And was famously competitive. He and Kunitz were friends, but he may have been trying to make Kunitz's book his own, his glory. James Dickey said that Roethke saw other poets as "rivals merely," with "appalling pettiness." Fixated on the kind of greatness that Koch mocks in "Fresh Air," when he redundantly intones, "Who are the great poets, and what are their names?" Koch is mocking, say, Stephen Spender in his poem from the era that begins, "I think continually of those who were truly great," who "left the vivid air signed with their honors." For years I misread "signed" as "singed" and liked the poem more.

...

His critics often have a similar emphasis. The question for future readers, one wrote, would be if Roethke was "truly great." Another worries that he lacks the "authentic greatness" of the greatly great modern poets. Another considers him "America's most major minor poet," an epithet that Roethke anticipated in a notebook: "I'm going to be a great man. A minor hint of a great man; but still great."

...

"Slight but unmistakable," Louise Bogan said of his work.

. . .

"A stricken minor soul," he said of himself.

. . .

As one who finds minor hints to be the most revealing, the most substantial, I'm less interested in the garish Mount Rushmores of poetic acclaim. I recently learned that it's not uncommon for poets my age to be seriously discussing which archive will receive "their papers." What ongoing world are they imagining.

. . .

His ambition could also be more inward-facing. "The trouble probably lies in the age itself," he wrote, of literary striving, "in the unwillingness of poets to face their ultimate inner responsibilities, in their willingness to seek refuge in words rather than transcending them."

. . .

His sense of identity was dependably mystical. "Jacob Boehme, like Roethke," one critic notes, "often referred to himself as a tree."

. . .

"I stretched like a board, almost a tree," he wrote.

. . .

And: "When I stand, I'm almost a tree."

. . .

And: "Is he bird or a tree? Not everyone can tell." I love the perspective of "not everyone can tell." Can the speaker tell? Can whoever he's responding to?

. . .

His reputation was often ruled by anecdote. The jocular tellings of bad behavior at the faculty club, impulsive purchases, schemes in the hydrotherapy tub. Drinking, pills. Delusions. Affairs. He often showed up with too many flowers, made guests stay too late. Suffered, was difficult, required care. The fur coats, baggy suits, what Richard Hugo called his "W.C. Fields-as-gangster" affectations. His knees hurt. But outside the anecdotes, I've strained to consider the hours reading, writing. The 277 notebooks in the archives, the annotations. He must have written for hours before any anecdote's party. How does that enter criticism. Picture the poet reading.

. . .

I was having trouble waking. Tumor, etc. Attempted to maintain my dogged scholastic diversion. I thought of

Barthes: "I shall punish myself, I shall chasten my body: cut my hair very short, conceal my eyes behind dark glasses (a way of taking the veil), devote myself to the study of some serious and abstract branch of learning. I shall get up early and work while it is still dark outside, like a monk. I shall be very patient, a little sad, in a word *worthy*, as suits a man of resentment." I shaved my head, walked to the archives.

. . .

Feeling fucked up, it's easy to feel like you must have fucked something up. Or everything. Or to assume this is just how things feel now. How they are. And so you think, you can at least make something—not of it, but through it. We might not pull through, but we might pull something through, a small knot in the frayed, if no great consolation. There's Fitzgerald, in "The Crack-Up": "I have now at last become a writer only."

. . .

Adrienne Rich: "The failure of criticism to locate the pain."

. . .

I wrote you as though by auto-fill fail, so you would think of me.

. . .

Roethke's poem "The Pure Fury" ("What book, O learned man, shall set me right? / Once I read nothing through a fearful night") goes on to show a time in which "every meaning had grown meaningless." It catalyzes a prowl:

> *That appetite for life so ravenous*
> *A man's a beast prowling in his own house,*
> *A beast with fangs, and out for his own blood*
> *Until he finds the thing he almost was*
> *When the pure fury first raged in his head*
> *And trees came closer with a denser shade.*

. . .

I first read those lines among trees near campus. Almost twenty years later, they were using the same sign to advertise the annual event: "The Physical and Spiritual Benefits of Tai Chi." I like what always applies.

. . .

And there was that wildness. I woke in a grove. A man asked if I had a light. Of course I did. He offered some of the foil he was smoking. I asked what it was. I couldn't understand the word.

[Setting:

This "Hugo Scene" (13) takes place in a car, somewhere in Pennsylvania. Probably near Philipsburg. Brad is in the way-back, facing out the back like a reference to Walter Benjamin. The audience could be in a car following. Or just in the passenger seat and regular backseat. The ventriloquist is driving.

The bumper sticker on the dashboard says, "Fractals Are Everywhere."]

HUGO SCENE, 13

and now it's time for Richard Hugo's *Death and the Good Life*…remember what he liked about noir was mostly mood…he rushes plot…he's making a frequency, in which certain things come through, that's the critical point…the lineage is frequency…

so the idea is Richard Hugo has turned forty and left the Seattle police force…he's past his prime in his prime…"I was forty" he says…"and I couldn't do anything else"…but his pension isn't enough… so he goes to Montana…small town deputy…

but there are some murders…axe murders…and the thing about Richard Hugo…I mean his character… this cop…Barnes…the thing about Barnes is…he *hates* murder…

> (BRAD *voice*) I was thinking about what you said…

about Barnes?…

> (BRAD *voice*) worms…

no it's Barnes…

> (BRAD *voice*) no about the worms…how they're fans of middles…you know what else is fans of middles…(*fanning self, maybe with hot dogs*

from pockets, one between each finger, like Wolverine)...fans...

I look forward to saying about you what Richard Hugo says about T. Curtoise Lamarr, the lackey...

(BRAD *voice*) what's that?

"he had been hurt for the last time"...

but even you will like this part...he finds the killer, solves the crime, but then there's another killer or maybe it's just another body...they keep finding the body...but it was axed differently...and this new axe was found in the snow...so he goes to Portland...I forget why but these people from Portland are involved...aren't they always...and one of them is the one who died so he goes to see them...

OK Brad I'll need you to play all these people...this is the crime Barnes turns up from 19 years ago...a second crime...rich Portland kids at the beach...a cold beach...start off as Dale Robbins and Joyce Cuddles Bebar and Lynn Hammer down at the beach...yes that's right and meanwhile back at the house...yes now be Candy Koski's body and also Lee Hammer coming in looking for...I forget what he said he was looking for but he comes in and finds Candy's body and is that...yes now be Vic Medici doing things to the body as was reported...oh but Vic Medici's lawyer...now be Vic Medici's lawyer...

Vic Medici's lawyer says it was artificial respiration trying to save her so make it that too...and the Portland jury believed him...of course someone's father planted an editorial in the Cannon Beach paper which biased the local community...so they had to have the trial back in Portland...

OK now get the axe again the axe...and as the body is being dragged away on the sled...this is the second body 19 years later...throw the axe in the snow...OK that was easy..."like getting Jimmy Carter drunk"...

now establish your alibi...that's right you were with Lynn Hammer the whole time...

> (BRAD *voice*) "some people are so absurd you just can't mistrust them"...

as Hugo said...then there's another twist...it's Manny Sanderson...now be Manny Sanderson... Manny Sanderson the creepy deputy with the weird eyes from Montana who Marnie seduced...he was the axe murderer actually not the first one who Barnes already found but the copycat...but Lee Hammer shoots him to cover it up because he's also doing things to the body of his twin sister Lynn yes...

and Barnes thinks it's all over and he's back in Montana and watching baseball and kissing his girlfriend over the phone which as he says isn't "sexy enough and you have to wipe off the mouthpiece afterward"...the price of ventriloquism...but he's also no longer distracted by Marnie or cars so he sees the twins on the same team trading uniforms because one is a better hitter...and it all comes together..."like seeing *Hamlet* shut down by the fire department"...

and he's been wondering if he's a wrong thing in a right world...or a right thing in a wrong world...but he realizes he's actually a thing and it's actually a world...he's a thing in a world...hello, thingy world...and calls Rick Petrov the damn fine detective in Portland who also writes poetry and together they listen to the dial tone remembering an afternoon in the office with the wall-length lounging figure when one said "smell her breath" and one leaned toward her mouth in the mural and a giant whiff of perfume spouts into his face...

> (BRAD *swigs perfume, sputters it out in a mist*)

hey, Brad...how come a Ferris wheel seems more still when it's stopped than a car does...

> (BRAD *voice*) easy...you can get out of a stopped car and walk...

THIRD LECTURE

Well, on the third night—what does it say in Genesis? Or are the nocturnal activities of creation not recorded? Or, perhaps, we can assume the basics of, you know, "the nocturnal activities of creation."

In any case, welcome to our third night! The dandelions will be even higher before we're through. Well, not higher than we'll be. I'm not the only one who ate all the brownies, right? Protect me if the roses attack. "These flowers are all fangs," as Roethke says.

I'm glad to try to redeem last night's discussion, and I should apologize for what happened after. We were all a little tired. To start, how about a contender for the most beautiful thing I've ever seen? How about Roethke's annotations of the poetry of Gerard Manley Hopkins? This is when I was in Seattle, in the archives, sick, pretending not to be sick.

Roethke's notes start in pencil, just inside the cover. A green volume. "I myself become interested in." He finishes the thought in ink: "images of speed." Let us now become interested in—images of speed!

> (*Projects an image of Keanu in* Speed. *Laughter.*)

If you know anything about Theodore Roethke, the critic

John Wain wrote in 1964, shortly after the poet's death—that's "Wain" with an "eye"—it's that he "grew up in and around an enormous greenhouse." The greenhouses started just over there, past the fence. There's a model upstairs. But Roethke's *poetry* grew up in and around his annotations of other poets, in the margins of their books, and of his own life, in his extensive notebooks. You can see them in that other greenhouse, the archives in Seattle. Critics have studied his jottings and fragments in light of the published work, considering what Robert Heilman called the "sizable informal variorum" that preceded each poem. But you can also work the other way, reading Roethke's poetry in light of his notebooks and annotations. That is, the variorum isn't just a fossil record of footprints and feathers that presaged fully realized species, but a lively biome in itself. His poems can be read as a further iteration of that notational method.

That is, an early critic complained that "one is frequently called upon to decide whether a particular line is governed by its relation to the poem as a unit or by its effectiveness as an epigram." Read the poems in relation to the notebooks—as extensions of the notebooks' variety and zip—and that's not a problem. "The finished works serve as prologue to the jottings," as Geoff Dyer said, though not about Roethke.

That liveliness is especially apparent in his annotations of Hopkins. These aren't scholastic preparations, they're poetic actions in themselves. Picture it. Roethke underlines, circles, diagrams. He pens references, reactions, etymologies, associations, potential revisions. The notes rollick, rove, seethe. This one seems written from the shoulder, this one from the elbow, this one while spinning. Three colors of ink, capillary pulse, thick weave. "I want you to see the music," he writes by one line. That gloss is also a charge. "Like looking at a musical score in the sky," he writes by Hopkins' poem "The Sea and the Skylark."

His annotations transmit like that, like "looking at a musical score in the sky." They're far from the "appalling pettiness" of grand ambition that, according to James Dickey, caused Roethke to see other poets as "rivals merely." It's closer to what Carolyn Kizer said, about his "absolute, pure, and unjealous devotion" to others' poems. But you can see what Dickey meant in his stiffer poems, with their Yeatsian aping, their self-conscious straining to match the "authentic greatness" of the heroic Modernists, as Harold Bloom—of course—put it. In contrast, his annotations of Hopkins show a mind made manifold in relation to another. Each page is like a generous garden gone to seed, to frenetic heaven, saturated and roiling. "Face wild sound and spill music till there's nothing left to spill," he writes by a poem. It's an assessment. It's an ambition.

I wish we had some stained glass here, and a tornado—that'd start to get at how those pages feel.

Reading, in Roethke's Hopkins, isn't an adjunct to what he calls, elsewhere, reason's "dreary shed," its "grubby hutch for schoolboys." It's a sensual performance. His annotations track "a music of ideas—the music with dissonance," as he writes by one poem. He's talking about Hopkins' music and his own. The notes can be blissfully tender. "One of the loveliest of human gestures," he writes by Hopkins' phrase "I kiss my hand." At "a love glides" (his underlining), he writes, "a Whitman word." But Roethke is also an exacting fan. "Too much use of double alliteration," he writes by "The Loss of Eurydice." He revises, subtly, tempering the consonance by varying the vowels. "He was all of lovely manly mold" becomes, in his edit, "And he was of lovely manly mold." "Of the best we boast our sailors are" becomes "Of the best we boast our seamen are." Each case tightens the drone. "Yet God that hews mountain and continent, / Earth, all, out" becomes, marvelously, "Yet God the mountain-mason, continent- / Quarrier, earthwright." It out-Hopkins Hopkins.

Elsewhere, Roethke offers terse verdicts. By one poem: "flat." At another: "A little heavy on the come-to-Jesus." At the line "My tempests there, my fire and fever fussy," he writes: "Worst last line." Nevertheless, he sides with Hopkins when the book's editor calls some of the poems "exaggerated," faulting their "naked encounter of sensualism and ascetism." Roethke quips in the margin: "There are those who like naked encounters."

Among these raucous notes, a few pages are remarkably

bare. By the poem that starts "No worst, there is none. Pitched past pitch of grief," Roethke made a single note: "This is the best of his poems, a cry against God, against fate: no wallowing in Christ, almost." This judicious assessment, ascetic among the carousing, is affecting because of its contrast with the ebullient bouquets of notes on most pages.

Gorgeous, all around. I wish you could see it. But I'm a poet, I wrote a lot of notes, but I forget to take photos. But can I tell you the most beautiful part? There's a *second* copy of the same edition of Hopkins in the archives. In it, Roethke began his ecstatic annotation again, not replicating, not refining—he wasn't preparing a teaching copy, or transferring his notes for a tidy version—he was going through the text afresh, alert, reading his reading, its transmission, performing a perpetually original encounter, bricolage of illuminated leaps. *This* is what reading looks like. "Color riot," he scrawls by one passage, on a page streaming with hues. The experience of reading, these annotations suggest, makes one akin to the "opaque vase" that Roethke describes in "The Shape of the Fire," which "fills to the brim from a quick pouring, / Fills and trembles at the edge yet does not flow over, / Still holding and feeding the stem of the contained flower."

Those are some lines that get quoted all the time, and for good reason. They show the poised trembling in his poems, that pulse, what I called "haunting" on the first night. We were all there, yes? Maybe we still are?

So, there you have it, my contender. Get to Seattle and check it out. It's like seeing the first perception of sunlight coeval with the invention of leaded glass. And there are other books he marked up. He swoons at Dickinson, declaring in one margin: "I will tie the world to me!" It's both paraphrase and personal statement. In a selection of Blake's poetry, he offers criticism, such as "felt the fierce beat of minor rhythms"—what pith!—and eccentric pragmatism, such as "dewy grass is not a place to stay." That's sensible. Kizer also said that Roethke's principal characteristic was his "love for other people's poetry." That's clear throughout his annotations, but it's kinetic and soaring in his copies of Hopkins. His notebooks match that energy, 277 of which are in the archives. They read his life—and the life of his compositional process—with similar intensity. The poem is your life. Who me? Hi there. His notes are both spectacular and mundane. They leap, they lull. Taking flight and marking time. Here's a sample from February 1943:

> *Shit-fingered shepherd.*
> *Only an intolerable sadness.*
> *A great comic hippo.*
> *A noodle.*
> *And we loved new houses. Watched them go up.*
> *The spinal cord of song.*
> *The neck gangrened with guilt.*

> *We make what we do not believe.*
> *For 34 years I've been conducting my own progressive school.*
> *Only a phase of mirror.*
> *Fat as herring. The sawdust, the stumps, the void.*
> *Wind vents / Technical names / A grated lemon*

You can read additional samples, selected and arranged, in *Straw for the Fire* (1974), edited by David Wagoner. But it's something else to see the entire spool. Anyway, it's undeniable that Roethke worked up drafts of poems in these notebooks. That's been explored by, among others, Don Bogen in his vital study *A Necessary Order: Theodore Roethke and the Writing Process*. (You can tell it might be an important book about Theodore Roethke whenever the title isn't, simply, *Theodore Roethke* or *The Poetry of Theodore Roethke*. That shows the limits of some of the critical contention with his work. Sylvia Plath, in contrast, gets titles like *Pain, Parties, and Work: Sylvia Plath in New York, Summer 1953* and *Out of the Cradle Endlessly Rocking: Sylvia Plath as Mother-Creator in Light of Julia Kristeva's Theory of Subject Formation*. Theodore Roethke gets *Theodore Roethke*.) Bogen and others have done that work, but it's also possible to read the notebooks, and Roethke's liveliest annotations, as showing central qualities of his poetics. That is, the notebooks don't just show the compositional record; they reveal dynamics of recursion, reiteration, variation, and refrain that are central to his compositional values. This observation can lead to fresh readings of his poetry. For critical assessments, it can help one avoid overly chronological or reductively psychosexual interpretations. It can also help us avoid over-emphasizing his much-anthologized trophy poems, or just doing critical walk-throughs, readings more closed than close. Those trophy poems can, instead, be seen as iterations of larger dynamics. At the same time, this approach is compatible with more inspired studies that focus on Roethke's sensibility, such as Jay Parini's book—don't fault the name—*Theodore Roethke*.

This point is simple. Consider a passage like the following, one of many like it in the notebooks. With it in mind, we can reconsider passages from the published poetry. This sample is cut from a whirling, longer riff:

> *The stunted geraniums*
> *Between gray curtains*
> *Above stunted geraniums*
> *Between gray grass*
> *Between gray curtains*
> *Showing geraniums*
> *yellow geraniums*
> *Between gray curtains*
> *Eyes blue and round*
> *Looked past geraniums*
> *Eye blue and round*
> *Between*

Where stunted
By a stunted geranium
Between soot-gray
From a stunted
By a stunted
And stiff gray
Near a stunted geranium
Between gray curtains
By a stunted geranium
Over a stunted geranium
Past stiff gray
Past a stunted geranium
Through stiff gray curtains

It goes on. If we view the notebooks as a record of nascent, burgeoning poems, this passage could be read as tinkering, refining, working toward the best words in the best order, as though each subsequent line replaces the ones that precede it. The poet is straining to get it right, we'd say. We might note that this passage is from February 1944, and so these notes could be read as foreshadowing a passage from his next published collection, 1948's *The Lost Son and Other Poems*. Perhaps this workmanship led to the voice in lines like, say, "Under the concrete benches, / Hacking at black hairy roots" from "Weed Puller." Or we could remember that Roethke, as Wagoner writes, "returned to completed notebooks, often after an interval of several years, and hunted for what he could use, recombining old and new images, lines, or whole passages on related themes." And so we could see these lines as preceding basically anything in his finished work. "My geranium is dying," he wrote in a collection published in 1958. "Her shriveled petals falling / On the faded carpet," he wrote in "The Geranium," published in 1964.

Or else, with a mind more to dynamics than to direct textual genealogy, we could see the notebook passage as highlighting a sensibility at the edge of glitch. It doesn't prefigure a realized expression in the published poems, but it shows Roethke grafting a phrase forward through a manner of stammer, which also preserves and extends from the preceding lines. The poet isn't just trying to get it right; he's performing a process of getting, of righting, of getting at it, being in it. "This shaking keeps me steady." I start to see that tendency, of repetition that revises slightly, even as it emphasizes and frames, throughout his work. "And that sound, that single sound." "And in this rose, this rose in the sea-wind." "In the green of my sleep, / In the green." "The flowers leaned on themselves, the flowers in hollows." "I'm one to follow, / To follow." "The present falls, the present falls away." I'm sure everyone here knows the technical term for this rhetorical form, so I don't need to.

And that's not even getting into all his emphatic doublings: "The cliffs! The cliffs!" "O Lull Me, Lull Me." "Unfold! Unfold!" "I Cry, Love! Love!" "This way! This way!" "I see what sings! / What sings!"

Such echoes and grace notes are present, I think, whenever we read. A phrase resonates off the page, and the mind lingers on a word, or stays with the aftertaste of a potential alternate phrasing, an initial misreading, a wondering, or we misremember in a way that says something about us, even while reading forward. Some poets, such as John Taggart and Shane McCrae and Gertrude Stein, show these echoes and variations overtly in the text. Roethke's notebooks are rich with that effect. His poems, though published in configurations that his readers would have seen more as "poems" than "notes," have it, too.

Here's why I think this matters: This revised way of reading Roethke downplays the critical centrality of moving set pieces like "My Papa's Waltz," which, as many term papers available for sale online demonstrate, tidily offers itself to certain kinds of reading. It also suggests that Roethke's most innovative, exuberant work, such as the sequences in 1951's *Praise to the End!* ("A deep dish. Lumps in it. / I can't taste my mother. / Hoo") has more in common with Armantrout and Ashbery than with the pat enactment of Freudian regression, as we discussed last night, or the night before.

This approach could seem to take Roethke out of his time and read him through ours, in which many recent books of poetry look more like his notebooks than like his poems. But it might also read him more accurately than criticism that labors to align his work with his life, obsessing over whether the arc of his poems is that of early genius to stately maturity, straining to consider if the vagaries of his life and writing hew to what Randall Stiffler called "the evolutionary, the disruptive, or the dialectical." Much of that scholarship reflects the work of early critics who were writing as each collection was released. They desired, as Stiffler observed, "the intelligibility that a sequence of historical events offers," even when it meant "sacrificing some perspective on his poetic project as a whole." But we can be free of that, at least tonight. We come with other histories. We buy *The Collected Poems* one afternoon in 2002 for $7.50 at Magus Books on 42nd Street. We open to any page. We read for lines, not for poems. We're not bothered by the badness of "The Lord God has taken my heaviness away"—a little heavy on the come-to-Jesus—because it's preceded by the groaning boast of "I am most immoderately married" and followed shortly after by "Being, not doing, is my first joy," which feels wise, at nineteen. We read from the need for lines. We find those two, and thrill at the mix of tones, and take them with us, moving like a jotting in the margins of our day.

[Setting:

The final "Hugo Scenes" (14–18) take place in a clearing in the Wissahickon Valley Park in Philadelphia.

It's summer. We got pastries at the train station café. There's a feeling of sweaty closeness and air. Someone is carrying a guitar.

Sitting next to someone, their head on your shoulder. You kiss their head. This friend.]

HUGO SCENE, 14

it's worth remembering that Hugo also wrote poems…that was the most real…what he said in prose was just what he said…when he wasn't writing poems…the poems say more…

the difference between poetry and prose…is prose…

tell me the whoosh the wind was invented to hide…

poems as wind…let it speak through…

he knew it came up a lot in his poems…wind…the word…all words are words for the wind…if he speaks of a town…he speaks of wind…that public utility…a public good…

he says "your vocabulary is limited by your obsessions. It doesn't bother me that 'wind' appears over and over in my poems"…it appears, becomes apparent…that means it isn't the subject…it appears in and through his subjects…a parent…as it were…

so I spent a season transcribing by hand degrees of wind in Hugo…a catalogue of instances…"we need the catalogue in our time," as Roethke wrote… he loved shopping…I read all of Hugo's poems in order…transcribed "wind" and the words around it…the first instance says who we are…

> *us wind. // We*

the collective self moves through "wind" from the object of "us" to the subject of "we"...the next occurrences elaborate...

> *in wind. The*
> *The wind / grew*

I preserved line breaks with a slash...stanza breaks with two...and punctuation...when it appeared...I became a detective of gusts...many of which were poems in themselves, such as...

> *by wind, pines*

or else they combined...I'm still moving in sequence here...

> *a wind bigger*
> *when wind caves*
> *gently. Wind touched*

translating Hugo back into wind..."windows" notwithstanding...nor "winnowed" nor "wild" nor "dwindle" nor "wine"...

> *the wind relaxed*
> *the wind drives*
> *eyes. // Wind is*

"world" notwithstanding...nor "weird" nor "wide" nor "warm mind"...

the wind and
a wind the
in wind—a
in wind.
than wind from
long wind, / killed
The wind will
and wind travels
the wind / and
and wind / repeats
foreign wind. // Fate
the wind, / her
in wind from
the wind / will
the wind remains
not wind, the
eyes, wind and
Good wind / mixes
the wind— / steelhead
new wind and
stars, / wind around
the wind, the
and wind into
the wind, / heard
and wind / by
the wind is
and wind is
in wind. / When
and wind are

> *when wind is*
> *summer wind.*

I ended on "wind" when poems did...the wind winding up like a field of telephones...unraveling like Roethke's notes...words to transmit the hum, a harmonic glitch we move in...echoing field... speaking through...ducks out of the fountain... moments becoming the whole greenhouse gone to pieces...glass shards in the garden...

> *much wind? / When*
> *now wind has*
> *British wind was*
> *the wind.*
> *the wind. / You*
> *the wind is*
> *high wind, ruins*
> *The wind is*
> *the wind / make*
> *the wind goes*
> *by wind. Sun*
> *south wind often*
> *by wind / that*
> *send / wind black*
> *is wind. // Let*
> *good wind. Harsh*
> *in wind, and*
> *and wind is*
> *of wind gave*

The wind / seemed
the wind. The
of wind I
their winds? Planes

"wink" notwithstanding...nor "wife" nor "won"
nor "vine" nor "mound" nor "crone" nor "void"
nor "cinders" nor "vie"...

the wind, the
ball / wind is
of wind, out
of wind.
by wind we
boiling wind / beside
the wind, wounding
the wind? This
calm / wind must
It's wind. / Morning
futile wind. This
and wind / have
enemy, wind, / helps
hear wind rubbing
alone. Wind had
throat, wind / and
for wind to
and wind would
the winds' slap
of wind: the
the wind. It

of wind across
This wind is
of wind / is
This wind has
and wind pours
the wind decides
obscure, wind / the
gross wind must
this wind and
one wind returning
me wind and
slightest wind.
by. / Wind is
hard wind— / no
the wind is
every wind. / Wave
Indian wind. My
degrading wind. / Sage
this wind / fakes
out. / Wind this
weakens wind / coming
Even wind must
open, wind is
no wind. The
no wind playing
the wind leak
arrogant wind. You
The wind is
The wind / is

in wind. V
The wind / takes
the wind will
way wind recommends
the wind, is
been wind / and
The wind had
to, / wind a
and wind. Black
teasing wind, when
every wind. Our
cruel winds. His
The wind at
The wind died
mute wind / deeds
the wind or
the wind I
as wind is
when wind stops
the wind against
And wind. Always
Always wind that
that wind, came
easy wind, came
easy, wind and
the wind changed
in wind and
the wind. Copper
like wind on

meadow wind. Stay
Wind deserted
the wind would
the wind / like
With wind high
second wind. / These
cooling wind low
this wind placated
by wind, the
more wind. / On
hot wind reeks
level wind / slanting
warning wind. / We'd
the winds we
those winds, over
to wind.
north wind white
to wind and
the wind. // I
and wind resolved
both wind and
hard wind we
cold winds. Right?
west wind brings
good wind he
The wind up
The wind / doesn't
or wind. They
this wind / in

*this wind / I'm
right wind right
just wind. I
need wind to
No wind here
God, wind. / I'll
in Wind. You
worship wind any
where wind slams
and wind are
this wind head
the wind / that
the wind acting
that wind
the wind is
the wind. // Your
pro-wind and
country wind shouts
of wind. I
painting, / wind blowing
hard wind blows
that wind. We're
The wind sang
same wind / Zen*

the wind in Hugo terminates in Zen…that's Zen Hofman…a friend of his…as the life and the books wind down…I find myself wanting him to say "wind" once more…

but before it ends...there's that one capitalized instance of "Wind" that's not at the start of a sentence...it's above as "in Wind you"...it appears in a poem shortly before he says "So what if it all burns out? It burns"...but before that he says "You found it in Wind. You don't worship wind any more"...tell me where you found it...and what you no longer worship...

HUGO SCENE, 15

I didn't read my favorite of his books for "wind"…
save one precious for later…let it wind me in time…

HUGO SCENE, 16

I like the notion of the jump bid…like in pinochle…when you don't have a good hand to bet…but you have a good hand to play…so you bet unusually high…which tells your partner to bet even higher…so you can have a chance to play your hand…I love hearing the unusual bets of others…poems and criticism are…the unusual bets of others…or their betting even higher in response to…what I said or what…we haven't yet heard…

oh, and I should've said…when I got lost in that meadow I'm permitted to return to often…this meadow I know well…it's because it was spring…I'd been going there all winter…and then in sudden lush spring…I had no coordinates…lost…in the lush heave…

spinning and caught and spinning and catching and spinning and catching and caught and spinning…

HUGO SCENE, 17

despite all that...I'm still sometimes asked to tell a personal story...like in a corporate improv retreat situation...shouldn't it all be obvious...everywhere we've been...the color of my eyes...is all those winds...

but they say tell us the most personal story...in your own voice...be for sale on that level...this is improv mandates from HR...

when I have to tell a most personal story like that...I always tell this story M. told me he heard on the radio about Neil Young...my most personal story... is a story my friend heard about Neil Young...

the improv people acting it out...weeping...

I tell them...I have this friend M....he is a very famous musician...you've heard his songs... sometimes even I don't realize it...for example Starbucks...or that ad for that new prescription we all have...

I was visiting his place in the mountains...his cabin and studio...

he played this song he'd just finished...here I might say something about his life...a recent divorce... new child...illness he survived...speaking in ways that make the HR trainers mouth along...

and this song was magnificent dearest freshness deep down wind...

but M. wasn't so sure...so M. says...M. says let's hear how it sounds on the lake...and I follow him down an even more fir-needle-lined path...our footsteps even more dearly freshly making velvet the wind...

and in the green canoe I thought he'd have a little speaker or boombox or just sing...he could've just sung...like Orpheus if Orpheus had actually believed in music enough...his music that had made creatures follow him...if Orpheus had believed in music enough to just sing and know Eurydice was following him and be assured...or if he had believed in her as a creature...

but instead M. touched this button on this other phone he had...this glowing one...

and all around us from one giant speaker on top of the cabin and one giant speaker on top of the studio...over the water the music...we heard it as the lake hears and I could feel it in the canoe and in the oars in my hands I mean in the trees the oars or my hands or our bodies had been...

HUGO SCENE, 18

but there are also times when I want to tell an actual personal story…or hear myself say it…

spinning and caught and spinning and catching and spinning…

for example there was this time…back when I had nothing but moments…when I decided to have a vision to help me…I prepared a jug of cucumber water and the dark room…like for developing a photo…or like the darkness of a diving bird's back…so predators looking down from above…into the darkness of the depths and the diving bird's back…see only depths…

and found myself and a friend standing at the shore…cold shore…Oregon Coast…toes in the water…logs and kelp in the waves…

I understood our friends were in the car behind the dunes…Cannon Beach…

and I understood I would need to swim out alone into the kelp and logs…

and you would return to our friends and drive away…sitting on a towel…as after any day at the beach…

in the vision you were touching my arm…saying

it's all right…and telling me yes I would need to swim out into the kelp and logs…in a dark t-shirt darkening…into the cold water forever…

saying it's all right…you will need to swim out into the kelp and logs into the cold water forever…which will be an end but it's all right…you will need to swim out…but it's all right…we can stand together in the surf before that…we can stand here as long as we have to…

"The ocean does that to me. It gives me license for all sorts of poses"…as Hugo says…

"When I got to the front, I could see the car still there and beyond it, about twenty yards, the Scotch broom. It was quiet. The surf sounded dreamy and far off. The slight wind moved sporadic grass faintly. The gray front was nearly overhead"…

the vision sustained me for years…it survived me… but my personal story…it happened much later… after the vision survived me and I had abandoned scholarship…I finally understood…I had been at that ocean…not in a vision but in my life…I had stood at the shore…with you and you and alone in this life…and I had come back from it…many times… ordinary as the day…I had been there all the time and come back…you don't worship wind anymore…

starfish and mist…thick anemones…on my lunch

break from the bookstore at actual Cannon Beach...reading for full shifts in the store...so at lunch I could just stare...

my bike in my co-worker's truck after work...leave me at our apartment under the Ferris wheel...that summer we put spinach in everything...called it "lace"...in that apartment overlooking the thin river past the dunes...river reversing with tide...we stared so long our first afternoon there...to understand its directions...

fishermen on the bridge...a winter sky that withholds and holds...

it took me a long time to understand...I had already been there...had already come back...

we can stand at the shore as long as we have to whenever we want...

and I fucking love the ocean...

ACKNOWLEDGMENTS

Grateful acknowledgment to the publications that first featured portions of this work, often in earlier forms, and to their editors: *Autofocus* (Michael Wheaton), *Coma* (Zach Peckham), *Georgia Review* (Gerald Maa), *Poetry Northwest* (Bill Carty). Thank you to the Vermont Studio Center for a fellowship that supported this project and to the librarians at Special Collections at the University of Washington Libraries. Thank you to the National Endowment for the Arts.

I'm especially grateful to Beatrice Roethke Lushington and the estate of Theodore Roethke for permissions.

"Caryl's Lecture" is written by Caryl Pagel. Thank you, Caryl.

Thank you, Alicia Wright and *Annulet*, for hosting the presentations "The Roethke Pretense, Parts 1 and 2" in the Linkages Lectures series.

Thank you again, Michael Wheaton, for including a portion in the anthology *If I Can Be Honest*.

Thank you, Michelle Taransky, for the form that inspired the wind section.

Thank you, Jess Barbagallo, Caren Beilin, Jonathan Crimmins, Henry Goldkamp, Michael Loughran, Alyssa Perry, Adrienne Raphel, Andalyn Young.

Thanks, Hilary.

Thanks, Justin, Sarah, Tommy. Thanks, everyone who first talked with me in Seattle about poetry, including Alex, Andy, Cass, Jay, Melissa, Rick, Sierra, Steven, Tyler.

Thank you, Kate Kremer and 53rd State Press. Amazing editor, amazing press.

Faculty development funds from the University of the Arts supported this project. The University of the Arts closed abruptly in 2024. My experiences working there (2013–2020) informed the book's thinking about higher education. Tribute to those working toward models that can serve our students and this moment.

I'm grateful to the Cleveland Institute of Art, and to my students and colleagues there, for offering one of those models and for funds that supported a research trip to Saginaw, Michigan, home of the Friends of Theodore Roethke Foundation. The foundation's work on behalf of the expansive legacy of Theodore Roethke is an inspiration. More information is at friendsofroethke.org.

SELECTED SOURCES

William Barillas, ed., *A Field Guide to the Poetry of Theodore Roethke* and *The Midwestern Pastoral: Place and Landscape in Literature of the American Heartland.*

Nicholson Baker, *U and I* and *The Anthologist.*

Peter Balakian, *Theodore Roethke's Far Fields.*

Richard Allen Blessing, *Theodore Roethke's Dynamic Vision.*

Harold Bloom, ed., *Theodore Roethke.*

Don Bogen, *A Necessary Order: Theodore Roethke and the Writing Process.*

Kenneth Burke, "The Vegetal Radicalism of Theodore Roethke."

Terence Cave, *Thinking with Literature: Towards a Cognitive Criticism.*

Geoff Dyer, *Out of Sheer Rage.*

Natalie Gerber's writing on intonation and prosody (including "Intonation and the Conventions of Free Verse").

Peter Gizzi, ed., *The House That Jack Built: The Collected Lectures of Jack Spicer.*

Richard Hugo, *Making Certain It Goes On: The Collected Poems of Richard Hugo*, *The Triggering Town*, and *Death and the Good Life.*

Walter Kalaidjian, *Understanding Theodore Roethke.*

Jenijoy La Belle, *The Echoing Wood of Theodore Roethke*.

Saikat Majumdar and Aarthi Vadde, eds., *The Critic As Amateur*.

Karl Malkoff, *Theodore Roethke: An Introduction to the Poetry*.

Ralph J. Mills, Jr., *Theodore Roethke*.

Aaron M. Moe, *Zoopoetics: Animals and the Making of Poetry*.

Lorine Niedecker, *Collected Works* (Jenny Penberthy, ed.).

Emily Ogden, *On Not Knowing: How to Love and Other Essays*.

Jay Parini, *Theodore Roethke: An American Romantic*.

Bernard Quetchenbach, *Back from the Far Field: American Nature Poetry in the Late 20th Century*.

Theodore Roethke, *The Collected Poems*, *On Poetry and Craft: Selected Prose*, *Straw for the Fire: From the Notebooks of Theodore Roethke* (David Wagoner, ed.), *Selected Letters*, and the Theodore Roethke Papers, Special Collections, University of Washington Libraries.

Allan Seager, *The Glass House: The Life of Theodore Roethke*.

Rosemary Sullivan, *Theodore Roethke: The Garden Master*.

Arnold Stein, ed., *Theodore Roethke: Essays on the Poetry*.

Randall Stiffler, *Theodore Roethke: The Poet and His Critics*.

David Wagoner, *First Class*.

CONTRIBUTORS

Zach Savich is the author of seven collections of poetry, including *Momently* (Black Ocean, 2024), and several chapbooks, limited-edition volumes, and books of prose. His work has received the Iowa Poetry Prize, the Colorado Prize for Poetry, the CSU Poetry Center's Open Book Award, and other honors, including residencies from the Vermont Studio Center, ArtPark, and the Chautauqua Institution. His writing has appeared in journals and anthologies including *American Poetry Review*, *Best New Poets*, *Boston Review*, *Georgia Review*, *Poetry Northwest*, and elsewhere. Savich teaches at the Cleveland Institute of Art and serves as co-editor of Rescue Press's Open Prose Series. He is a 2025 recipient of a fellowship in Creative Writing from the National Endowment for the Arts.

Caryl Pagel is the author of four books, most recently *Free Clean Fill Dirt* (poetry, University of Akron Press) and *Out Of Nowhere Into Nothing* (essays, FC2). She is currently working on a book about the Great Lakes and Lorine Niedecker.

53rd State Press publishes lucid, challenging, and lively new writing for performance. Our catalog includes new plays as well as scores and notations for interdisciplinary performance, graphic adaptations, and essays on theater and dance. For more information or to order books, please visit 53rdstatepress.org.

53rd State Press books are represented to the trade by TCG (Theater Communications Group). TCG books are exclusively distributed to the book trade by Consortium Book Sales and Distribution, an Ingram Brand.

A Field of Telephones is made possible by the New York State Council on the Arts with the support of the Office of the Governor and the New York State Legislature.